MODERN
BALLET

John Percival

MODERN BALLET

HARMONY BOOKS

New York

Copyright © 1970 by John Percival

Revised edition Copyright © 1980 by John Percival

Revised edition first published by
The Herbert Press Limited, 65 Belsize Lane, London NW3 5AU
Designed by Pauline Harrison

This edition first published in the United States by Harmony Books, a division of
Crown Publishers, Inc., One Park Avenue, New York, New York 10016

Published in Canada by General Publishing Company, Ltd.
Printed in Great Britain

Library of Congress Cataloging in Publication Data
    Percival, John
        Modern ballet.

    Includes index.
        1. Ballet.   2. Ballet—History.   I. Title
    GV1787.P4 1980   792.8'09'04   79-23705
    ISBN 0-517-54094-0
    ISBN 0-517-54095-9 pbk.

FRONTISPIECE Robert Cohan
Waterless Method of Swimming Instruction (Downes) LCDT
Photo: Anthony Crickmay

Contents

Introduction

Dance is the fastest-growing and possibly the fastest-changing art today. Much of what is being performed now would have been unimaginable even a few years back. Even those aspects of ballet which look superficially much the same have mostly undergone important changes of performing style and presentation.

Ten years ago, in a book with the same title as this one, I tried to give a brief, simple account of the artistic revolution taking place in the world of dance. That revolution has continued to such an extent that, to bring the account up to date, the book has needed not merely extending but completely rewriting.

Technique has changed and, more important, the whole approach of a generation of choreographers, dancers and audiences has changed too. The cumulative effect of the changes is that what used to be thought a pleasant but trivial entertainment (although it did sometimes develop ideas above its station) has increasingly become an art form comparable with music, painting and drama in its ability to interest and move the spectator. I try to show here how that has happened and to put it in its wider artistic context. But to understand what has happened lately, it is first necessary to go further back, and see the seeds of subsequent developments planted almost unnoticed at the time. What has happened since then has been, for those of us who watched it, a source of surprise and delight. I think these qualities are going to continue.

The background

During the 1950s, ballet in Russia, the United States and Britain (then, as now, the main centres) seemed to be developing along set lines.

The Russians, after much experiment in the early years of Soviet rule, had settled for a monumental kind of dance-drama that was easy to follow, spectacular in its effects and popular. Even the old classics, still in favour for the virtuoso technique they showed off and the attractive music they used, were revised on similar lines, emphasizing their dramatic content and giving it an uplifting aspect. In *Giselle*, for instance, they stressed the redemption of the heartless aristocratic hero through the selfless love of the peasant girl who died because of his faithlessness.

In Britain, those same ballet classics were the mainstay of the repertory, staged as faithfully as possible to the original choreography but usually without much sense of theatrical presentation and with standards of performance that, although improving, reflected British ballet's lack of any long tradition. Except for one great ballerina, Margot Fonteyn, and two outstanding choreographers, Frederick Ashton and Antony Tudor (both of whom came to fame in the 1930s), the British companies had few claims to international attention. The modern repertory, generally small in scale, took second place to the classics in popularity and playing time.

Things were different in America, thanks to another long-established choreographer, George Balanchine, who directed a series of companies, from the American Ballet in the 1930s to New York

City Ballet, founded in 1948. Although full recognition of his importance came later, Balanchine, an émigré Russian, already dominated the American scene. Only one American-born choreographer, Jerome Robbins, showed promise of real stature. The main rivals to New York City Ballet were primarily imitations of the earlier Ballets Russes tradition, based on a combination of the classics, usually in abbreviated versions, and works from, or in the manner of, the Diaghilev company which had popularized ballet in the west during the first third of this century. Curiously, British ballet in its formative years showed far less direct Diaghilev influence, going instead to the fountainhead of the imperial Russian tradition from which Diaghilev himself sprang.

It needs to be remembered that ballet in Britain and America was still young. In both countries it effectively started in the 1930s, enlarged and matured during the 1940s, and was in a period of consolidation during the 1950s. There was a limited amount of cross-fertilization, notably when Tudor, one of the early leaders of British ballet, went to live in America. During the decade 1946–56 American Ballet Theatre and New York City Ballet both played several seasons in Europe, and from 1949 onwards the Sadler's Wells Ballet (later the Royal Ballet) made regular visits to north America.

The great leap forward began at Covent Garden on 3 October 1956 when the Bolshoi Ballet from Moscow opened its first season in the west with Galina Ulanova dancing in *Romeo and Juliet*. Suddenly British and American ballet were faced with a challenging new standard of comparison. Ulanova was generally recognized as the greatest dancer of her day, but the qualities she possessed were found in some degree all through the company. The ballet itself, with choreography by Leonid Lavrovsky, took the old kind of dance-drama to its furthest peak. Audiences were overwhelmed by an intensely dramatic style of dancing, whole-hearted in its presentation. The male dancers swept and soared across the stage in an unrivalled way, and the partnering introduced acrobatic tricks to extend the expressive range of the dance. Subsequent visits to Britain and America by this company and the Kirov Ballet from Leningrad (a more elegant and reticent, even more 'aristocratic' company, but still in the same tradition) confirmed the impression of the first season. Western companies had to respond.

The first result was direct imitation. The best of the younger dancers managed to emulate some of the Russian tricks, especially in

Jean Coralli (1779–1854) and Jules Perrot (1810–92)
Giselle (Adam) Bolshoi Ballet production by Leonid Lavrovsky

Leonid Lavrovsky (1905–67)
Romeo and Juliet (Prokofiev) Bolshoi Ballet
Sergei Koren, Alexei Yermolaev

OPPOSITE *Giselle* (Bolshoi Ballet)
Galina Ulanova, Nikolai Fadeyechev

partnering; others had to follow. One indication of this effect is the
way ballerinas are no longer lifted only to shoulder height by their
partners, but customarily held high above the man's head at the full
stretch of his arms, or even on one arm. This was introduced into
Russian ballet by the choreographer Feodor Lopukhov and attacked
by one critic as 'more gynaecology than ballet' but its greater effec-
tiveness has won universal acceptance.

Tricks came first; later, this extended technique was used for
dramatic purposes as choreographers, especially the younger ones,
tried to bring into their work the seriousness and humanity they saw
in the best of the Russian ballets. The Russians in turn, although to

a limited extent, tried to adapt for their own purposes qualities they found in the west, especially the use of dance more than acting to tell their stories.

While these waves of influence flowed east and west, another current began to make itself felt. Its first lappings were apparent even sooner, when the American modern dancer Martha Graham brought her company for a London season in 1954. A few people greatly admired her work but audiences were tiny. That was true of a later tour by a company headed by José Limón with the noted choreographer, teacher and theorist Doris Humphrey as artistic director. Not until 1963, when Graham enjoyed an unprecedented success at the Edinburgh Festival, did this tide really gather strength.

Such is the background to the changes that have taken place in ballet. Some of the changes flow directly from those events; others were influenced by developments in the other arts or in society generally; some were brought about by a single gifted person. The important thing was that dance had been made ready for new developments.

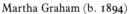

Martha Graham (b. 1894)

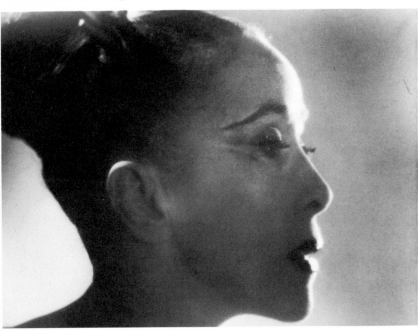

A new heart for ballet

The importance one creative and strong-minded person can have is shown by the way one major company alone has remained largely unaffected by the changes taking place all around it. This is New York City Ballet, and the explanation is the almost autocratic power exercised by its chief choreographer and artistic leader, George Balanchine. Born in St Petersburg, educated at the Imperial Ballet School there, a choreographer (and a revolutionary one, too) from the beginning of his career, Balanchine left Russia in 1924, soon made a name, and was invited in 1933 to organize a school and a company of American ballet from which, after many vicissitudes, his present company grew.

In sheer quantity Balanchine dominates the ballet scene throughout America and western Europe. He has created more than 150 ballets; between forty and fifty of them are in the active repertory of New York City Ballet – a stock constantly renewed by new creations. Others are danced by at least a dozen leading European companies and several companies in north, south and central America. No other choreographer has ever had so many ballets performed so widely or so often.

Nobody reaches such a position without remarkable gifts. Balanchine can turn his hand to almost any kind of ballet: his favourite comparisons to explain his work are with the craftsmanship of a carpenter or the skill of a chef, both making what the customer wants. But he has little interest in using dance to tell a story, though the early *Prodigal Son* and later reworkings of *Harlequinade* and *The Nutcracker* demonstrate his ability in that line.

The beginnings of his greatness can be traced to his oldest surviving

work, *Apollo* (1928). In this, the simplicity and muscular strength of Stravinsky's music encouraged the young choreographer to aim at similar qualities. The ballet achieved an austere beauty that has proved timeless; Balanchine characteristically emphasized the supremacy of music and dance by progressively paring away the décor in subsequent revivals. In *Apollo*, the strict academic technique was partly remoulded to suit the theme, the score and the dancers for whom it was made.

OPPOSITE George Balanchine (b. 1904)
Harlequinade (Drigo) New York City Ballet
Edward Villella

George Balanchine
Apollo (Stravinsky) New York City Ballet
Patricia Wilde, Jacques d'Amboise, Jillana
Photo: Martha Swope

That is fundamentally the way Balanchine has worked ever since. Most of his work nowadays falls into either of two categories. On the one hand he uses the old virtuoso classical technique for ballets of sheer dance display, sometimes mistily romantic, more often brilliant, with

George Balanchine
Vienna Waltzes (Johann Strauss the younger, Lehár, Richard Strauss)
New York City Ballet
Photo: Martha Swope

perhaps a dash of humour or showmanship besides. Each of these works takes its flavour from the music, chosen with a taste that embraces Gershwin, Gottschalk or Sousa equally with Bach, Gluck or Mozart. Ravel has been a special favourite, and a great success lately was *Vienna Waltzes*, which reflects that city's popular artistic heritage from Johann Strauss the younger, through Lehár to Richard Strauss. Balanchine even experimented with something approaching a three-act plotless ballet when he made *Jewels* – three related settings of symphonic music by Fauré, Stravinsky and Tchaikovsky.

Stravinsky's recent music, however, has more often served Balanchine for his other favourite form, in which the old open, straightforward bravura style is changed into a highly personal manner with turned-in feet, bent arms and legs, unexpected quirks, twists and bends of the body, and rhythms that sink or rise in a surprising way. First seen to illustrate the theme of *The Four Temperaments* (to commissioned music by Hindemith) in 1946, this style was developed by Balanchine as a way of setting abstract dances to contemporary music. *Agon* (Stravinsky, 1957) is the best-known example: tense, sinewy, brief and compressed, with an unexpected underlying humour. Webern, Charles Ives, Yannis Xenakis and others have been treated in this way, as well as many other Stravinsky scores, the *Violin Concerto* being one of the most characteristic examples with its two terse duets.

George Balanchine
The Four Temperaments (Hindemith) New York City Ballet
Arthur Mitchell

OPPOSITE George Balanchine
Agon (Stravinsky) New York City Ballet
Suzanne Farrell, Peter Martins

What makes Balanchine's work outstanding is, first, his flair for making his dancers look attractive in movement; secondly, his unsurpassed understanding of music as a basis for dance. Those qualities, sustained over the years, give his company homogeneity and have gradually led to recognition of its supremacy, certainly in America and arguably anywhere in the world today. He himself has developed (lately, for instance, he has turned increasingly to a genre he formerly avoided, the long spectacular ballet occupying an evening on its own) but his developments spring from within.

New York City Ballet in 1959 partly anticipated, apparently without realizing the implications, one of the trends of the next decade. Deciding to present a ballet to Webern's complete orchestral works, Balanchine and his general director Lincoln Kirstein invited Martha Graham to undertake part of the choreography with her own company as guest artists. The resulting ballet, *Episodes*, as its name implies was not a real collaboration. Graham's part was a story-ballet about Mary, Queen of Scots. Balanchine produced a series of dances in his inverted-classic manner and incidentally introduced another modern dancer, Paul Taylor, for a specially made solo. *Episodes* remained in the repertory but without the modern dance sections, and years later Graham revived her section for her own company. They were never again given as a whole, but the occasion marked the coming together of traditions, classical and modern, which had been thought incompatible.

At this time, however, the main influence on classical ballet was still the cross-fertilization of the Russian and western schools. With the Royal Ballet, John Cranko's *The Prince of the Pagodas*, produced only three months after the Bolshoi season at Covent Garden, was already full of the high Russian-style lifts. He was later to make a duet in that style actually called *Hommage à Bolschoi*.

Cranko was one of the choreographers who went on to a deeper understanding of the Russians' underlying approach. His *Antigone* (1959) showed no direct stylistic Russian influence; in fact the choreographer he was most affected by at that time was Jerome Robbins. But the content of *Antigone*, an impassioned plea for an individual stand

George Balanchine
Episodes (Webern) New York City Ballet
Mimi Paul, Anthony Blum
Photo: Anthony Crickmay

John Cranko (1927–1973)
Prince of the Pagodas (Britten) Royal Ballet
Svetlana Beriosova, David Blair
Photo: Tony Armstrong Jones

against war, reflected the dissatisfaction with trivialities which followed exposure to the seriousness and dramatic intensity of the Bolshoi Ballet. He had always been concerned with important issues beneath an entertaining surface triviality: the Russians themselves recognized this in *The Lady and the Fool*, which the west had regarded only as a comedy. The Bolshoi influence gave him the opportunity to make this explicit. Later, just before his early death, he turned his gifts to implied criticism

John Cranko
Antigone (Theodorakis) Royal Ballet
Photo: Reg Wilson

of the Russian régime in *Traces*, a ballet about the effect of imprisonment in a totalitarian society made when he was much concerned about the situation of Valery and Galina Panov, dancers prevented from leaving Russia.

Cranko was able to develop his ideas freely when he moved in 1961 to take charge of the Stuttgart Ballet, which under his direction became within a few years one of the world's leading companies. Part of their

23

John Cranko
Jeu de Cartes (Stravinsky) Stuttgart Ballet
Egon Madsen
Photo: Werner Schloske

OPPOSITE John Cranko
Onegin (Tchaikovsky, arr. Stolze) Stuttgart Ballet
Marcia Haydée, Ray Barra
Photo: Werner Schloske

success came from the way he built a true ensemble in which the stars (all built up within the company) and supporting dancers worked as a strong team with a sense of purpose. Equally important was the reper-tory he developed.

His short ballets included devastatingly uninhibited comedy, not-ably in Stravinsky's *Jeu de Cartes*, and also highly experimental pieces in which he was much influenced by other arts. *The Interrogation* was inspired by Francis Bacon's paintings. In *Présence*, to music by the avant-garde composer Bernd Alois Zimmermann, his three leading characters were archetypal figures from literature, Molly Bloom, Don Quixote and Ubu Roi, representing aspects of man's nature: sexual, idealistic and earthily opportunist. *Présence* was unusual in presenta-tion as well as theme, with enigmatic passages of dancing interspersed between explicit mimed scenes.

Yet Cranko was also a traditionalist, mounting for his company a series of large-scale narrative works on which their success chiefly rested. These included *Romeo and Juliet*, *Onegin*, *The Taming of the Shrew* and a completely new *Swan Lake* with a genuinely tragic ending:

John Cranko
The Taming of the Shrew (Scarlatti, arr. Stolze) Stuttgart Ballet
Egon Madsen, Susanne Hanke
Photo: Anthony Crickmay

the wicked magician triumphant, the prince drowned and Odette still transformed into a swan. Cranko was the supreme choreographic story-teller of his day, finding a way to narrate his stories entirely in dancing. Through such works he developed his dancers until his Brazilian-born ballerina Marcia Haydée became one of the finest dancers anywhere, equally great in tragedy (Juliet or Tatiana) or comedy (Kate in *The Shrew*).

Kenneth Macmillan (b. 1929)
Das Lied von der Erde (Mahler) Stuttgart Ballet
Marcia Haydée, Ray Barra, Egon Madsen
Photo: Alo Storz

Cranko's Royal Ballet colleague, Kenneth MacMillan, was similarly affected by the Bolshoi visit and turned from the artificial drama of his early ballets to subjects like *The Invitation* which tried to show credible characters in an explosive situation: a boy and girl involved sexually (and for the girl disastrously) with an older couple. When the Covent Garden direction refused MacMillan's wish to choreograph *Das Lied von der Erde*, Mahler's mighty score for singers and orchestra, because they thought the music unsuited to ballet, Cranko invited him to produce it at Stuttgart instead. Cranko's *Opus 1*, to Webern music, was premiered the same night and had the same theme: man's brief life, the inevitability of death but the continuance of life itself. Both ballets, MacMillan's on a huge scale, Cranko's a miniature, were original, powerful, poetic and moving.

MacMillan in turn directed a German company, the Ballet of the Deutsche Oper, Berlin, for three years from 1966. His most important creation there, *Anastasia*, was a dramatic exploration of the mind of a woman who claimed to be the surviving member of the Russian imperial family. With Lynn Seymour as the heroine, the ballet used a soundtrack as well as music, incorporated films as part of its action and crowded a nightmare realism into its formalized action. Sadly, the effect was swamped when, after becoming director of the Royal Ballet in 1970, he converted it into a three-act ballet with two Tchaikovsky symphonies and much distorted Russian history preceding the original drama to music by Martinù.

While Cranko, MacMillan and others responded to the stimulus of the Russian challenge, some companies subjected themselves to a more direct Russian influence. Vladimir Bourmeister, who had been in charge of the Stanislavsky Ballet in Moscow, was invited to stage his famous production of *Swan Lake* at the Paris Opéra in 1960. It tried to adapt the story as a struggle between good and evil, and had a spectacular last act incorporating an illusion of actually flooding the stage. The following year, Bourmeister created a new three-act ballet, *The Snow Maiden*, for London Festival Ballet. Based on a Russian folk tale and using Russian folk dance as well as Soviet-style classicism for its choreography, it was an ambitious and at least partly successful attempt at importing the Russian style complete. Later, Bourmeister mounted the ballet in Moscow.

Another Russian-born choreographer, Vaslav Orlikovsky, already working in Germany and Switzerland, became more prominent about that time. He too staged several works for Festival Ballet, including a

ABOVE
Kenneth MacMillan
Anastasia
(Tchaikovsky, Martinù)
Royal Ballet
Lynn Seymour, Adrian Grater,
Marilyn Trounson
Photo: Anthony Crickmay

LEFT
Vladimir Bourmeister
(1904–1971)
The Snow Maiden (Tchaikovsky)
London Festival Ballet
Oleg Briansky, Marilyn Burr
Photo: Anthony Crickmay

Vakhtang Chabukiani (b. 1910)
Othello (Machavariani) Tbilisi Ballet
Bekar Monavardissashvili, Zurab Kikaleishvili
Photo: Serge Lido

big production of *Peer Gynt* which proved very popular for a while, and a lavish *Cinderella* for a specially formed company in Paris.

The greatest Russian influence on the west was in the staging of the classics. Denmark alone maintained its own nineteenth-century tradition with the ballets of August Bournonville. Elsewhere, except in Russia (where a larger selection of Petipa's ballets survived at least in fragmentary form), companies wanting a traditional basis for their work relied almost entirely on five ballets, all of them either created or substantially revised in St Petersburg in the late nineteenth century by Marius Petipa or his assistant Lev Ivanov. They were *Giselle* and *Coppelia*, both adapted from French originals, and the Tchaikovsky ballets *Swan Lake*, *The Sleeping Beauty* and *The Nutcracker*. Those five ballets dominated the international repertory from San Francisco to Vladivostok, from Stockholm to Cape Town, to an extent explained by, but out of all proportion to, their enduring merits of plot, music and dance. Once the Stanislavsky *Swan Lake*, the Bolshoi *Giselle* and the Kirov *Sleeping Beauty* had been seen in the west, ideas about the most suitable stylistic and dramatic approach to these works began to change. Sometimes the ideas were only half digested and the results disastrous; several leading companies put on new versions of the classics and hurriedly dropped them again. But expectations were now higher and they began to be met, especially when a further generation of Russians came to the west and started mounting productions.

The traffic in ideas between Russia and the west was not only one way. Inside Russia the old monumental, solidly plotted kind of production continued. An example of its merits was *Othello*, mounted by Vakhtang Chabukiani in 1957 for the company he directed at Tbilisi. An uneven work, it was distinguished by the heroic ambitiousness of its theme and its striking incarnation of the leading characters, a bold impetuous Othello and a surly disdainful Iago, outwardly bluff but

Yuri Grigorovich (b. 1927)
The Stone Flower (Prokofiev) Bolshoi Ballet
Ekaterina Maximova, Vladimir Vassiliev

insinuatingly dangerous. About the same time, however, Yuri Grigorovich staged a new production of *The Stone Flower* which began a fresh trend in Russian ballet. Prokofiev's *Stone Flower* had previously been unsuccessful in a traditional production by Lavrovsky, the creator of *Romeo and Juliet*. Grigorovich reconceived it as a series of dance episodes telling the story in dance terms without old-fashioned mime. In this form, the ballet was successful enough to be staged, after its Kirov premiere, also in Moscow, Novosibirsk and Stockholm.

Grigorovich's inspiration for this approach came primarily from the veteran (and at that time partly discredited) choreographer, Feodor Lopukhov, who had been responsible in the early days of the revolution for preserving the classical heritage, which he regarded as a necessary basis for any experiment, and also for many innovations. Lopukhov was, together with Ulanova and the choreographer and folk-dance director Igor Moiseyev, one of several prominent people dissatisfied with the heavy emphasis on content in Russian ballet at that time. They wanted greater concern for form on the one hand and expressiveness on the other. Those ideas were reinforced when Grigorovich and other young Russian artists had their first chance to see a ballet by Balanchine, his brilliant display piece to Bizet's *Symphony in C*, performed by the Paris Opéra Ballet on a Russian tour. This was much admired, and so were other works (especially *Episodes*, so unlike anything the Russians had seen before) when New York City Ballet went to Moscow and Leningrad in 1962. Nobody in Russia actually copied Balanchine's completely plotless style until much later, but Asaf Messerer's *School of Ballet* came close to it. This virtuoso display piece, based on a ballet class, was a special case, because it originated in a period Messerer spent as guest teacher in Brussels and was then mounted for the Bolshoi at the suggestion of the American impresario Sol Hurok, being premiered during an American tour. That same year, 1962, also saw the production of Kasyan Goleizovsky's *Scriabiniana*, a highly inventive suite of unrelated dances to Scriabin music, marking the rehabilitation of a choreographer long out of favour. The previous year, Igor Belsky staged *Leningrad Symphony*, which treated the German invasion and siege in abstract dance terms. In Russia, too, things were changing.

Meanwhile the first stirrings of other trends began to be felt. An abysmally bad ballet created in Paris in 1958, *Le Rendezvous manqué* (toured to Britain and America as *Broken Date*), deserves mention only as an augury of better things to come. The use of fashionable celebrities from outside ballet, Françoise Sagan as author and Roger Vadim as

Igor Belsky (b. 1925)
Leningrad Symphony (Shostakovich) Kirov Ballet
Oleg Sokolow

producer, proved a dead end, but the work was an innovation in trying to make ballet appeal to a popular audience. In London, for instance, it played in a large theatre normally used as a cinema.

Roland Petit's *Cyrano de Bergerac*, also given a commercial run in Paris and London, was a similar attempt soon afterwards at putting on a popular show in the form of a ballet; later this formed part of Petit's film *Black Tights* which, with commentary by Maurice Chevalier, was clearly aimed at a general audience. Petit, directing companies first in Paris and more recently in Marseilles, has continued to put on ballets of pure entertainment, notably a sophisticated updating of *Coppelia* (himself playing Dr Coppelius as a cross between Chevalier and Fred Astaire) and a powerfully melodramatic adaptation of Victor Hugo's novel *Notre-Dame de Paris*. They have alternated in his output, however, with more esoteric productions including one, *Les Intermittences du Coeur*, ambitiously based on Proust's series of novels.

A choreographer who has gone even further in building a mass audience is Maurice Béjart, a man of enormous daring and enterprise. After running his own small company, he staged Stravinsky's *Rite of Spring* in 1959 for the Royal Theatre in Brussels with such success (thanks partly to its uninhibited sexuality) that he was invited to form a larger company based there which has gone on to tour world-wide. Its grandiose and challenging title, the Ballet of the Twentieth Century, is characteristic. Aiming largely at young people, Béjart pioneered gigantic spectacles which were given in vast auditoria, including one built for his needs in Brussels. (There and in Paris he became almost a pop star, with fans buying posters of his photograph and chanting his name after each performance).

To Beethoven's *Ninth Symphony* and the Berlioz *Romeo and Juliet* he expresses themes of universal brotherhood, deliberately using dancers of many races and different colours. *Firebird* in his treatment becomes a propagandist fable of revolutionary guerrillas. But he does not depend on obvious popularization. He is equally able to match the mysticism and the avant-garde techniques of the composer Karlheinz Stockhausen in *Stimmung*, and when he pursues special themes that interest

34

Maurice Béjart (b. 1927)
Firebird (Stravinsky) Budapest Ballet

him, such as eastern religions or homosexuality, he has the flair to strike a responsive chord in many of his audience. Some of his works reflect his interest in spoken drama and song as dance; among them are *Notre Faust*, in which he builds a kind of philosophical autobiography on Goethe's play, mingling Argentine tangos with a Bach mass for the

score, and *Le Molière Imaginaire*, made for the Comédie-Française and based on their great playwright's life and works.

Béjart can be disconcertingly banal in his actual choreography, although he has a gift for making good solos and his dancers are often of exceptional quality. His provocative subjects and iconoclastic treatment find a response among audiences who would never be interested by more traditional styles; but in Britain, and even more in the United States, his approach often infuriates followers of traditional ballet.

Maurice Béjart
Stimmung (Stockhausen)
Ballet of the 20th Century
Jorge Donn, centre
Photo: André Biro

The possibility of appealing to both general and specialized audiences is shown by the career of Jerome Robbins. From the start, he worked in the commercial theatre as well as ballet. His first ballet, *Fancy Free*, formed the basis of the musical *On the Town*. Later, after working with both American Ballet Theatre and New York City Ballet, Robbins conceived and directed *West Side Story*, which enjoyed widespread success in both stage and screen versions.

In 1958 Robbins started his own company, Ballets:USA, originally for appearances at the first Festival of Two Worlds in Spoleto and at the Brussels World Fair. A tour of Europe and a New York season followed, but thereafter the company performed only sporadically and disbanded in 1962. Two works which Robbins created for them proved influential, both to symphonic jazz scores by Robert Prince. *NY Export, Op. Jazz* was the more popular, presenting a portrait of rather violent big-city life in almost abstract form. *Events*, although more specific in its contents (a homosexual encounter, the rise and fall of a Negro entertainer, the failure of religion), left many people puzzled

ABOVE AND OPPOSITE Jerome Robbins (b. 1918)
NY Export, Opus Jazz (Prince) Ballets: USA

about its total implication. But both works used a jazz-flavoured version of classical dancing that was revolutionary in catching the cool detachment as well as the energy of American life. The dancers, in sneakers and jeans instead of the soft slippers and tights of traditional ballet, conveyed a feeling of a specifically American, specifically contemporary way of life. The company's repertory also included one of the funniest ballets in years, *The Concert*, parodying conventional responses to music. Robbins is one of the few choreographers who can be funny just as well as he can be serious.

Robbins's long estrangement from ballet after disbanding his company was a source of bitter regret, but when he returned (after work on Broadway, also a period of theatrical experiment) it was with no loss of impact or originality. *Dances at a Gathering*, to a Chopin piano score (1969), is simply a series of dances for a cast of ten, lasting more than an hour, but the craftsmanship of its invention and shaping to the music,

Jerome Robbins
Dances at a Gathering (Chopin) New York City Ballet
Jean-Pierre Bonnefous, Patricia McBride, Robert Maiorano, Susan Pilarre
Photo: Martha Swope

together with the play of relationships implied, though never explicitly stated, among the dancers, made it immensely admired and widely imitated. In *Watermill*, influenced by Japanese Noh techniques (and also by the work of the theatre director Robert Wilson), he produced an extraordinarily slow piece in which a man looks back on his life. Several of his recent works have been on a large scale, including a ballet to the whole of the *Goldberg Variations*. From his early interest in character ballets he has moved mainly to classicism, although the jazz influence on his classicism shows again in his setting of Ravel's *concerto In G major*.

The adaptability and durability of Robbins illustrates the way a few really fine choreographers continue for many years to dominate the world of ballet. Balanchine is another such and so is his contemporary Frederick Ashton.

As choreographer and for seven years director of the Royal Ballet,

Antony Tudor (b. 1909)
Shadowplay (Koechlin) Royal Ballet
Anthony Dowell
Photo: Donald Southern

Ashton proved able easily to assimilate changing fashions (as in the pop-art designs of *Jazz Calendar* or the psychedelic lighting of *Sinfonietta*) without neglecting more enduring qualities. Under his direction, the company's repertory became more adventurous, including two creations by Ashton's old colleague Antony Tudor, whom he persuaded from his American exile. One of these, *Shadowplay*, used an unlikely combination of a situation from Kipling's *Jungle Book*, a treatment from oriental sources and modern French music for a calm, quiet allegory of a boy growing up. The other, *Knight Errant*, was an explicitly bawdy comedy based on *Les Liaisons Dangereuses* which disappeared far too soon from the programmes.

Ashton himself could create from the simplest means: in *Monotones* he made a ballet of limpid beauty with just two trios of dancers, starkly simple costumes, Satie music and a bare stage. He could also transform the unlikeliest material, as in *Enigma Variations* where, avoiding what could have been an embarrassingly fulsome parade of characters, he concentrated on the noblest aspect of Elgar's music and created for it a unique expression in dancing of the quality of friendship. Ashton was also one of the first to reveal an understanding of the special qualities of Rudolf Nureyev when he left the Kirov Ballet in 1961 for a career in the west, his dramatic departure hitting the headlines from which he has seldom been absent since.

Nureyev soon became, for many years, closely associated with the Royal Ballet, and *Marguerite and Armand*, made by Ashton for him and Fonteyn, was the first and is still perhaps the best work created for him. Nureyev's presence provided an experience new for a western company, that of a Russian dancer, and an exceptional one at that, actually alternating roles with its own male dancers, although the Royal Ballet did have a Bolshoi-trained ballerina, Violetta Elvin (Prokhorova) for ten years from 1946. Some of the British male dancers suffered from his arrival but the long-term effect on both technique and presentation was beneficial, especially when Nureyev began to produce ballets for the company, starting with an act of Petipa's *Bayaderka*.

One unforeseen result of Nureyev's advent was a new lease of life for

Frederick Ashton (b. 1904)
Marguerite and Armand (Liszt) Royal Ballet
Margot Fonteyn
Photo: Frederika Davis

Fonteyn. Since Ulanova's retirement, she and Maya Plisetskaya of the Bolshoi shone above all rivals, but now there were small signs of a possible end to her supremacy through declining technique and confidence. Nureyev changed all that. Responding to his highly charged stage presence, Fonteyn found a dramatic power that had previously eluded her. In place of the formerly reserved, carefully balanced dancer emerged a woman who threw herself impetuously into her roles. Consequently, she went on to many more years of recognition as a unique artist. The old Fonteyn could never have impersonated successfully the impassioned courtesan Marguerite, although equally the Fonteyn of later years could no longer dance a lyrical-classical role like the one created for her (by the same choreographer) in *Symphonic Variations*, which therefore passed to a younger generation.

Frederick Ashton
Marguerite and Armand
Margot Fonteyn,
Rudolf Nureyev
Photo: Houston Rogers

Frederick Ashton
Symphonic Variations
(Franck) Royal Ballet
Antoinette Sibley
Photo: Rosemary Winckley

August Bournonville
The Conservatoire (Paulli) Royal Danish Ballet
Photo: Von Haven

August Bournonville (1805–79)
Napoli (Paulli, Helsted, Gade and Lumbye) Royal Danish Ballet
Niels Kehlet, Solveig Østergaard, Inge Sand
Photo: Rosemary Winckley

Nureyev was not the only famous male dancer to appear as guest at Covent Garden in 1962. Erik Bruhn was invited too, both to dance and to stage two short pieces by Bournonville. Danish by birth and training, Bruhn was brought up in the light, crisp, easy but exact style which Bournonville learned in Paris early in the nineteenth century and fostered in Copenhagen as leader of the Royal Danish Ballet for nearly fifty years. During that time he built up a repertory of masterpieces which remained almost unknown outside Denmark but were preserved there all the more lovingly because no other choreographer even

approaching similar stature arose within the company. Bournonville
had always hoped for fame abroad but never found it. Three quarters of
a century after his death, he at last won a posthumous international
reputation when *La Sylphide*, extracts from *Napoli* and *The Conservatoire* and some shorter divertissements were mounted all over Europe
and America by Harald Lander (former ballet director in Copenhagen),
Bruhn and others. With them, and with Nureyev's classic revivals too
(*Raymonda* and *Don Quixote* followed *Bayaderka*), the choice of classics
became much less restricted.

Peter Darrell (b. 1929)
The Prisoners (Bartók)
Western Theatre Ballet
Simon Mottram, Elaine
McDonald, Peter Cazalet
Photo: Anthony Crickmay

Peter Darrell
Mods and Rockers
(The Beatles)
Photo: Bob Johnson

At the same time, various people working within the classical ballet tradition were trying to extend its scope. They tended to work mainly in small companies: the Robert Joffrey Ballet in America, for example, and Ballet Rambert in Britain, both of which were transformed by subsequent developments and are therefore discussed later. Especially enterprising was the work of another small company, Western Theatre Ballet, formed at Bristol in 1957 in an attempt to give Britain a regional company. Lack of local support soon forced them into the usual touring circuit, but the company held to another of its intentions, of using the classical ballet technique in a more dramatic and entertaining way. Peter Darrell, the resident choreographer and artistic director, achieved this in their very first programme with *The Prisoners*, about a gaol break followed by murder which leads one of the escapers to find he has only exchanged one prison for another at the hands of a woman who shelters and dominates him. Darrell has a flair for comedy too (usually of a dark kind) which kept the company going through sticky patches, and his *Wedding Present*, about a marriage ruined when the wife finds her husband had a homosexual lover, proved one of the few ballets to achieve true tragedy rather than pathos. *Mods and Rockers*, based on pop dances and set to Beatles music just as they were about to change from children's idols to international figures, gave the company wide popularity. In 1966, Darrell created the first full-evening British ballet with a contemporary setting, *Sun into Darkness*. This ballet, about a village carnival turning almost accidentally into an orgiastic ritual murder, introduced new ideas in presentation. A playwright, David Rudkin, wrote the plot and Colin Graham, a theatrical and operatic director, was involved with the choreographer at all stages of preparation. This innovation (repeated in some later works) helped stimulate a dramatic flair and feeling for ensemble playing in the dancers – a quality that inspired Jack Carter, an experienced and versatile choreographer, when he made *Cage of God* for them, interpreting the fall of man as a rather sinister practical joke by the Almighty.

But Western Theatre Ballet's achievements were won against the tide, which by the 1960s was beginning to flow fast towards a different kind of dancing that questioned the supremacy of, even the need for, the long-established classical tradition.

Peter Darrell
Sun into Darkness (Williamson) Western Theatre Ballet
Simon Mottram, Donna Day Washington
Photo: Anthony Crickmay

A new way of dancing

The name 'modern dance' is awkward and ambiguous but I must use it for want of any better to describe the kind of dancing evolved in this century as an alternative to classical ballet. The word modern grows more questionable all the time in this context, since the movement can be traced back certainly as far as Isadora Duncan and other equally revolutionary but less famous dancers who flourished at the beginning of the century. Duncan's free style was based partly on imagined Greek antiquity and served more as inspiration than model for those who came after, although one or two of her pupils' pupils are still able to demonstrate the fascination of her methods and the quality of her choreography, even without her own personality to illuminate it.

There was also a more tense style developed in Germany which flourished in the 1920s and 1930s and even today has not quite died out, although its influence now is extremely limited except in the surviving productions of its best practitioner, Kurt Jooss, whose most famous work, *The Green Table*, has sadly never lost its topicality as an attack on the politics of war since its premiere in 1932.

For practical purposes, most modern dance today springs from pupils of one of Duncan's American contemporaries, Ruth St Denis, and her partner (also husband) Ted Shawn. Their Denishawn School flourished, first in Los Angeles, then in New York, for about fifteen years from 1915. Among the most prominent pupils were the leaders of the next generation, Martha Graham, Doris Humphrey and Charles Weidman, who all formed their artistic policies by reaction against the simple movement interpretations of music they had been taught.

In their generation, modern dance was primarily a solo art. In contrast to classical ballet, where the dancer must acquire the accepted technique and style, the creators of modern dance tried to evolve a technique and style to fit their individual gifts. What makes Martha Graham pre-eminent is the quality of her own dancing and choreography; but what makes her so influential is that from her experience over the years she evolved a technique that could be codified and taught by progressive daily exercises in the same way as classical ballet. It is based on a simple idea, the tension between opposites: balance and falling, or the contractions and stretching involved in breathing. To teach this comprehensive and consistent method she had evolved, Graham established a school in New York. The economic circumstances of modern dance were such that her company could usually perform for only a few consecutive weeks at a time. Between seasons, she and her leading dancers could support themselves by teaching at the school; several of

Kurt Jooss (1901–79)
The Green Table (Cohen) Dutch National Ballet
Photo: Maria Austria

Martha Graham
Letter to the World (Johnson) Graham Dance Company
Martha Graham, Robert Cohan

the dancers also got together their own performing groups at intervals
to dance their own choreography.

Graham's work developed from an attempt to give physical expression to inward feelings. That is true even of the richly inventive series of
almost abstract group ballets she made for dancers of her company.
Diversion of Angels, for instance, carries definite moods and makes
much of contrasts between the personalities of its soloists, one girl

lyrically ecstatic, another gravely serene. In *Acrobats of God* she used one of her own classes as the basis for a delicately funny work with the dancers toiling away, herself moving among them in search of inspiration and her rehearsal assistant literally cracking a whip over everybody. In structure, this echoes the rituals, evoking primitive societies or religious mysteries, which were the basis of works like *Primitive Mysteries* or *Dark Meadow*. She often treated specifically American subjects, notably in *Appalachian Spring* and her Emily Dickinson ballet *Letter to the World*. Many of her works have attempted to analyse the thoughts, fears and dreams of a mythological, historical or biblical person. These dance dramas were usually built around her own gifts as a performer, and with advancing years (she was already sixty by 1954, her first London season) she tended to make the central role less arduous, a woman looking back at life. Typical Graham subjects are the Freudian *Night Journey* (the Oedipus legend with Jocasta the main character), a startlingly sensual *Phaedra*, the biblical *Legend of Judith* with its horrifying picture of Holofernes's head rolling in a blanket, and *Errand into the Maze*, where the Minotaur became the basis of an exploration of deep-seated human fears. But she also produced *Seraphic Dialogue*, based on various aspects of Joan of Arc (as maid, warrior and martyr, finally becoming St Joan) which, although some passages reflected terror or frenzy, was fundamentally joyous in its mood. Her biggest work, *Clytemnestra*, is a three-act exploration of the whole Theban myth, as gripping as it is ambitious.

When Graham had to give up dancing through ill-health, her company closed, but her soloists kept the school going and she eventually resumed activity, passing on her own roles to a younger generation. The new company has a more accomplished and athletic technique than the dancers who grew up with Graham artistically, but without the passionate intensity of their predecessors. That intensity was recaptured by Nureyev when he appeared as an occasional guest with the company from 1975, the year Graham created *Lucifer* with him in the title part.

OPPOSITE ABOVE Martha Graham
Seraphic Dialogue (dello Joio) Graham Dance Company
Ethel Winter, Linda Hodes, Helen McGehee, Yuriko

BELOW Martha Graham
Clytemnestra (El-Dabh) Graham Dance Company
Martha Graham, David Wood

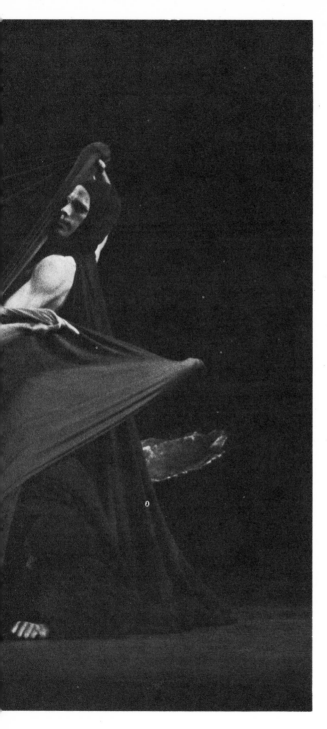

Martha Graham
Lucifer (El-Dabh)
Graham Dance Company
Rudolf Nureyev
Photo: Martha Swope

Erick Hawkins (b. 1909)
with Lucia Dlugoszewski

OPPOSITE Merce Cunningham (b. 1919)
Place (Mumma) Cunningham Dance Company
Merce Cunningham

Most of the leaders of the next generation of American modern
dancers graduated through Graham's company. Erick Hawkins, a
former ballet dancer who became her first partner, left to pursue his
own experimental path, creating works based on a calm flow of movement, usually in collaboration with a composer, Lucia Dlugoszewski,
and a sculptor, Ralph Dorazio.

Merce Cunningham, Graham's next partner, has had his own company since 1952 and for most of that time has been the most distinguished figure, as creator and performer, in modern dance. A dancer of
rare control, timing and authority, he too collaborated consistently with
certain composers and painters, but in his case they were themselves
outstanding although controversial artists: John Cage as musical director and other composers associated with him, Robert Rauschenberg,
Andy Warhol and Jasper Johns as designers. Cunningham's creative
powers matched theirs.

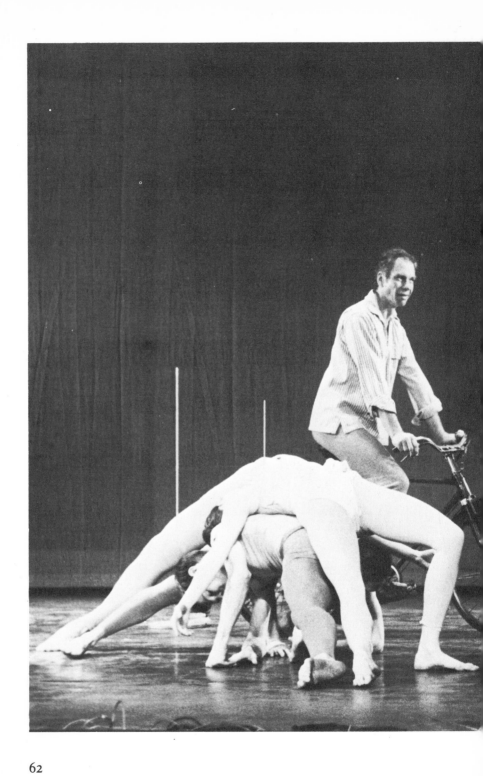

Merce Cunningham
Variations V (Cage)
Cunningham Dance Company

Collaboration in this instance may be a misleading word, because it was fundamental to their way of working that the various elements in their creation must each be self-sufficient, with dance not depending on music or vice versa. So although sound and movement generally occupy the same period of time, they are independently created and not rhythmically or emotionally related.

Cage's theories of composition involve elements left to chance. In *Variations V*, his music was controlled in performance by the dancers' movements haphazardly affecting photo-electric cells around the stage. Cunningham similarly introduced chance into some of his dances, either as an element in composition (tossing a coin when a choice was required) or even in a few works allowing the dancers a measure of choice in performance.

The result was that no two performances were alike: one example, *Story* (so called because it had none) could be funny one night, frightening another. It risked misfiring completely but could take on a tension and dramatic effect from unplanned qualities that might never have been found consciously. Rauschenberg improvised scenery during the action, even painting a picture on stage during one run of performances, adding a bit each night.

The use of chance elements attracted more attention than the seriously composed elements in Cunningham's work. But audiences attracted by his notoriety discovered a choreographer with the virtue of taking nothing for granted. His ballets could be outrageously funny (in *Antic Meet* he became involved with a sweater that had four arms but no neck), coolly beautiful (like *Nocturnes*, to Satie music) or inexplicably but terrifyingly tragic, like *Winterbranch* with its images of bodies falling, crawling or scurrying in darkness lit only by flashing beams. Objects took on importance in his work, so did light or darkness, silence and almost unbearable noise.

Always inclined to dispense with plot or character in his dances, Cunningham has grown increasingly to present them not in the form of set structures but as 'events' in which a collage of solos, duets or group dances from his previous works is danced. Each event lasts about ninety minutes and the chosen extracts may be short or long, being put together with an appearance of informal ease yet with a skill and taste that enables them to build to a climax and gently die away again.

Others who began their career with Graham include Anna Sokolow and Paul Taylor. Sokolow has generally treated themes of loneliness and despair, evolving an idiom that influenced Robbins in some

Merce Cunningham
Winterbranch (Young) Cunningham Dance Company
Carolyn Brown
Photo: Jack Mitchell

respects. Taylor has a far wider range, from surrealist humour in *Three Epitaphs* (vaudeville-style dances performed in ghoulish black costumes to music by a brass band) to the mysterious dark rites of *Runes*, from the blithe lyricism of *Aureole*, with music by Handel, to the hazardous bravura dancing he builds out of simple walking or running to Bach music in *Esplanade*. A slightly macabre humour appears often in his work, whether in a satirical piece like *Cloven Kingdom*, where four men in tail suits start dancing like monkeys, or in the more bitter mood of *Dust*. Himself formerly a dancer of unusual pliancy, he has since he stopped dancing continued to challenge some of the best young dancers in his company with his choreography.

One of the few major figures of his generation not associated with Graham was José Limón, a pupil of Graham's contemporary Doris Humphrey. After her performing career finished, Humphrey became artistic director of Limón's company until her death in 1958, and its joint choreographer with Limón. The company's characteristic style was a more sculptural one, leading to a heroic and dignified, but still expressive, manner in works like *Lament for Ignacio Sanchez Mejías*, based by Humphrey on García Lorca's poem about the death of a bullfighter, or Limón's *The Moor's Pavane*, a formal dance for four people with the passions of Othello, Iago, Desdemona and Emilia burning just below the surface. (This work, like Taylor's *Aureole*, has often been danced by ballet companies as well as modern dancers). Humphrey also founded a modern dance performing company for students of the Juilliard School, New York, and Limón was associated

OPPOSITE Paul Taylor (b. 1930)
Aureole (Handel)
Royal Danish Ballet
Photo: Von Haven

RIGHT Paul Taylor
Esplanade (Bach)
Taylor Dance Company
Photo: Rosemary Winckley

BELOW José Limón (1908–72)
The Moor's Pavane (Purcell)
Royal Danish Ballet
Bruce Marks, Toni Lander,
Vivi Flindt
Photo: John R. Johnsen

with attempts in the mid-sixties to establish a permanent repertory company for modern dance in America, presenting the work of many choreographers. Some years after his death the Limón company, maintained by his pupils, itself developed in that direction.

This was an unusual idea in the modern dance world, although the usual practice in ballet. One modern dance company that accomplished it was Alvin Ailey's American Dance Theatre. Besides his own works, the most notable of which is the beautiful and moving *Revelations*, a suite of dances to spirituals, Ailey also presented dances by his teacher Lester Horton (a cramped but impressive talent), Sokolow and Talley Beatty among others. Beatty's explosively dramatic *Road of the 'Phoebe Snow'* dealt with ghetto life behind the railway tracks, with affection destroyed by sexual violence and jealousy exacerbated by poverty. Of special interest were revivals of works by some of the pioneers of American dancing, including Ted Shawn. Unfortunately, Ailey the serious artist, concerned with social issues and building a choreographic repertory, had to contend with Ailey the show-biz entertainer who introduced an element that, although itself highly polished, swamped the company's other aims.

It is a curious thing that these and other American modern dance companies before the 1970s enjoyed only limited (although enthusiastic) support in their own country until they had first conquered the indifference to modern dance of the London audience. After that, their standing at home increased enormously and this contributed to the more secure basis for their work which was established over the following decade, enabling them to progress beyond the limited audience which had restricted them to brief off-Broadway seasons and to tours of the 'college circuit' of universities throughout the United States, especially those with an active theatre arts faculty.

Graham's and Limón's visits to London in the 1950s had excited a few people but they played to nearly empty houses. A fanatical admirer of Graham, Robin Howard, raised guarantees to bring her in 1963 to the Edinburgh Festival and for a London season. Taste proved to have caught up with her and she enjoyed a wild success, especially with dancers, artists and theatre people on whom her innovations exerted an influence such as she had never known before. The impact of her season was consolidated the following year when Cunningham, Ailey and Taylor all brought their companies to London.

Several qualities shared by these choreographers attracted the enthusiasm of a young audience. The way they showed off the individual qualities of their dancers, the direct human interest often found in their themes, and the way they related to current developments in the other arts all appealed, especially to those who found themselves out of sympathy with what they considered the artificiality of classical ballet. To meet the enthusiasm he had himself contributed to evoking, Howard launched an appeal (and contributed the greater part of his own possessions) to set up a school of contemporary dance in London, initially with Graham as artistic adviser. Robert Cohan, one of her principal dancers, was put in charge of the school and then of the company, London Contemporary Dance Theatre, that grew from it.

The rather tentative first season was given as early as 1967 and included work by David Earle, a Canadian who went home to become one of the founders of another Graham off-shoot, Toronto Dance

Robert Cohan (b. 1925)
Cell (Lloyd) London Contemporary Dance Theatre
Photo: Anthony Crickmay

Robert Cohan
Waterless Method of
Swimming Instruction
(Downes) LCDT
Photo: Anthony Crickmay

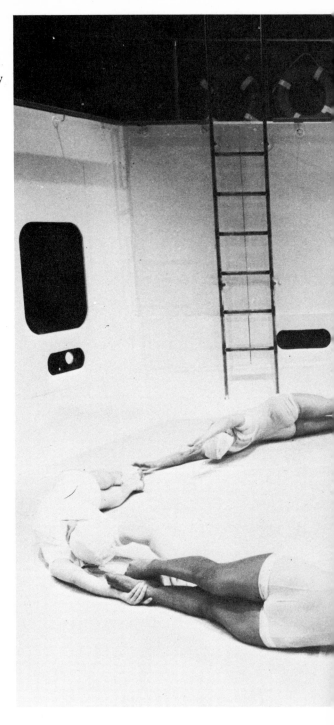

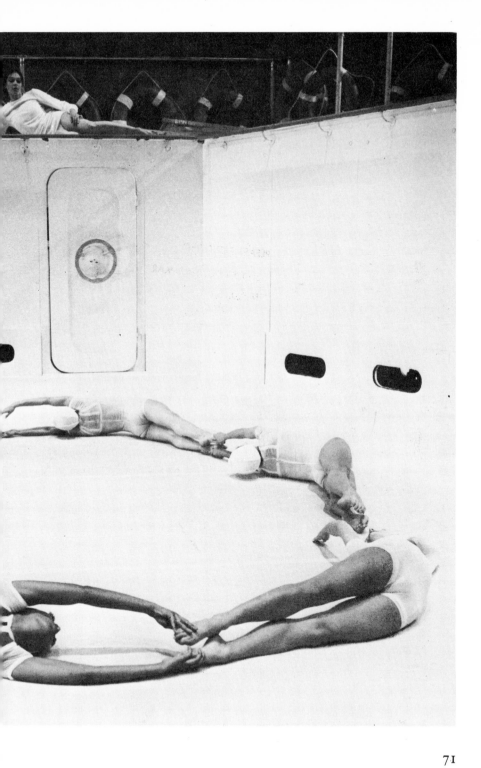

Theatre. By 1969 the company was ready to start regular performances. Guest dancers who had worked with Graham at first dominated the programmes; Cohan, Noemi Lapzeson, William Louther and Robert Powell. But only two of Graham's own ballets were given, *El Penitente* and *Diversion of Angels*, both of them for limited periods only. Several other guest choreographers were invited, but from the start the aim was to build a distinctively British repertory and thus give the company its own character.

Cohan provided the bulk of the creations; a flair for production enhances the impact of his sometimes conventional choreography, and he achieved striking theatrical effects in his best works such as *Cell*, *Stages* and *The Waterless Method of Swimming Instruction*, all of them with excellent designs (by Norberto Chiesa, Peter Farmer and Ian Murray Clarke respectively). The best of the young choreographers who arose within the company, Richard Alston, soon went off to found his own group, but Siobhan Davies revealed a gift for individual movement invention and Robert North (whose earliest works were made jointly with Noemi Lapzesou) showed an unusual ability for choosing interesting collaborators and treating subjects in a theatrical way. Later, another of the dancers, Micha Bergese, also began to demonstrate an original although often obscure approach to choreography. The way London Contemporary Dance Theatre, within a decade, built its own repertory and eager audience, and was able to undertake several foreign tours besides, was the most striking, but by no means the only evidence of the way modern dance was putting down roots in many places where it had never flourished before.

New ideas, new methods

While many people were trying to extend the expressiveness of classical ballet, and others fell directly under the spell of the established modern dancers, there were some whose response was more roundabout. In their many different ways, they had a vast effect on dancing: other people's as well as their own.

One early development was the attempt, pioneered in the Netherlands but soon copied elsewhere, to combine classic and modern traditions in one company. This was not quite unprecedented (Yvonne Georgi, who directed one of the earliest attempts to plant a dance tradition in Holland, had tried something of the sort), but Netherlands Dance Theatre was the first company to aim successfully at the highest standards in both techniques. It was founded in 1959 by a small group headed by an American teacher and choreographer, Ben Harkarvy, who was joined as artistic director by a young Dutch choreographer, Hans van Manen.

Starting with almost no resources except the unusual dedication of its members, Dance Theatre adopted a creative policy whereby every work in the repertory was by a living choreographer (something usual in modern dance but rare in ballet) and almost all were specially made for the company. With an average of ten new ballets a year, the dancers were constantly stimulated by new roles and only the best works needed to be retained in the repertory.

The early repertory included *Carmina Burana*, by the American choreographer John Butler to Carl Orff's rumbustious choral score (a classical version of beat music); the passionate frenzy of the dances made this the company's meal ticket, guaranteeing full houses wherever it was given. But Dance Theatre's artistic prestige in its first decade depended more on another American, Glen Tetley, who became for a time co-director. *Pierrot Lunaire*, one of his earliest ballets, illustrates his complex approach, with cross-references to *Petrushka* (which was written in the same year as Schoenberg's score) and a development of the struggle, traditional in the theatre since Roman days, between the white clown of innocence and the dark clown of experience. The

Glen Tetley (b. 1926)
The Anatomy Lesson (Landowski) Netherlands Dance Theatre
Jaap Flier
Photo: Anthony Crickmay

underlying meanings were implied within a series of lively and often wrily amusing dance images.

Most of Tetley's creations for Dance Theatre continued this allusive style. Notable were *The Anatomy Lesson*, in which Rembrandt's painting inspired a marvellous role for Jaap Flier, and *Sargasso*, in which another exceptional dancer, Willy de la Bije, played a woman becalmed in unsatisfied longings. In *Circles*, to Berio's music, and *Small Parades* (Varèse), Tetley turned to a plotless form, but *Arena*, a work for male

Glen Tetley
Circles (Berio) Netherlands Dance Theatre
Willy de la Bije, Jaap Flier

dancers only, continued his love of mixed meanings; its action, inspired by a pre-Columbian ball court Tetley had visited, was capable of being read equally in terms of the adventures of Theseus or modern athletes in a changing-room.

A work created jointly by Tetley and Hans van Manen, *Mutations* (1970), became for a time a provocative symbol of Dance Theatre's work. One of its themes was the contrast between dancers encumbered with high-soled buskins or tights as stiff-jointed as armour and others free of all clothing; of course the latter attracted most attention and it was soon known as 'the nude ballet'. It was not a true collaboration; Tetley was responsible for the stage action and Van Manen for film episodes which recurred at intervals: these introduced another kind of mutation, with some of the dancing being shown in extremely slow motion.

Harkarvy initially provided the more obviously classical side of the repertory, but gradually Van Manen's ballets came to assume that function, not so much for their technique as for their strong sense of form, manifest even in early works like the Stravinsky *Symphony in Three Movements* and his *Essay in Silence*. He set himself specific formal problems: *Five Sketches* emphasized the effort (usually concealed) that

Glen Tetley
Arena (Subotnick)
Netherlands Dance Theatre
Frans Vervenne, Jaap Flier
Photo: Rosemary Winckley

goes into dancing; in *Solo for Voice* (to John Cage's music) the singer, on stage, seemed to incite and provoke the two dancers, who were made to appear completely preoccupied with their cool mating ritual. *Situations* took place within a room built in the centre of the stage, lined with giant graph-paper and fitted with a digital display clock to make the spectator more aware of space and time. Although his early inspiration came

ABOVE
Glen Tetley and
Hans van Manen (b. 1932)
Mutations (Stockhausen)
Netherlands Dance Theatre
Photo: Anthony Crickmay

LEFT
Hans van Manen
Situations
(Music for film-makers)
Netherlands Dance Theatre
Leon Koning
Photo: Jennie Walton

largely from Balanchine and Robbins, Van Manen's interest in the visual arts helped develop the maturity he revealed in *Grosse Fuge* (1971) to Beethoven's music.

Jaap Flier, when he turned to choreography, was also much influenced by the other arts: *Elkesis* was based on the work of the Greek sculptor Takis, with six of his musical sculptures providing the accompaniment, some of his light-signals the décor (supplemented by actual street traffic-lights, wired to make their speed of operation and their brightness unpredictable), and with the movement also based on the principles of attraction and release that operate Takis's kinetic sculptures.

For many years, Netherlands Dance Theatre managed to preserve the balance of classic and modern; then modernism took over entirely for a while with the work of many American guest choreographers, followed later by a reaction to a more classical style.

Other companies which tried to follow Dance Theatre's lead also found themselves eventually tending towards one or other of the styles they tried to reconcile. The Joffrey Ballet of New York managed the mixture for a while, its best-known experimental work being Joffrey's *Astarte*, a multi-media ballet of deliberately sensational qualities. To music by a raga-rock group, Crome Syrkus, a male dancer, left a seat in the stalls, went on stage, stripped to his briefs and danced an erotic duet with a girl he found there, while filmed images of them on a screen behind dwarfed them both. Finally he walked away under the back-cloth and the film showed the supposed continuation of his journey, through the car park behind the theatre still nearly naked but attracting no attention. The ballet's fierce assault on the senses through loud music and blinding lights, its unexplained but compelling images and its mood related to current pop art and drug-taking met the spirit of the time and made it a great hit.

Joffrey's chief choreographer, Gerald Arpino, also pursued topical tendencies in works like *Trinity* and *Sacred Grove on Mount Tamalpais*, perhaps also in *Clowns*, which used those generally amiable beings for an allegory of man destroying himself through war. But Arpino continued to work in a wide range of styles (his *Viva Vivaldi!* and *Olympics*

Robert Joffrey (b. 1930)
Astarte (beat music) Joffrey Ballet
Nancy Robinson, Christian Holder
Photo: Herbert Migdoll

were popular display pieces) and the balance of the company's policy later moved to more traditional lines with emphasis on revivals of selected works from the historical or international repertory.

In Britain, the long-established Ballet Rambert remodelled itself consciously in 1966 after Dance Theatre's example. The exigencies of touring had made it difficult, perhaps even impossible, to maintain any longer its old pattern of performing a mixture of classics and of the splendid repertory of specially created works by all leading British choreographers which it had built up over three decades. The costs of running a large orchestra and a corps de ballet forced a crisis, and a new formula was proposed by Norman Morrice, a dancer in the company who, since his choreographic debut eight years earlier, had made one work a year (all the experimentation Rambert could afford). With him as associate director, the company reduced itself to a small ensemble of soloists and set off on consciously creative lines.

Morrice's own ballets had always shown a strong involvement with real life, including an attack on authoritarianism in *The Travellers* and a study of how dancers' lives and work react on each other in *Conflicts*. He brought the always interesting content of his ballets under greater formal control in *1–2–3*, a work of sculptural beauty and musical sensitivity about the birth of man and his doomed struggle for love, and in *Blind-Sight* used the contrast between blind and sighted characters as a metaphor for closed and open minds. *That is the Show* (to Berio's Sinfonia) treated the idea of heroes and their womenfolk, in myth and modern life, including a memorably tragic performance in the central role by Sandra Craig.

Morrice invited Tetley to work with the company; revivals of *Pierrot* and other works, and the creation of *Ziggurat* and *Embrace Tiger and Return to Mountain*, helped develop its morale. *Tiger*, based on the movements of T'ai-chi, a form of Chinese callisthenics meant for health, relaxation and defence, achieved a fascinating play of emotions through dances mixing stillness and aggression.

Other choreographers soon began to emerge within the company. John Chesworth showed a strong theatrical flair and original ideas in

Gerald Arpino (b. 1928)
Clowns (Kay) Joffrey Ballet
Robert Blankshine
Photo: James Howell

80

LEFT Norman Morrice (b. 1931)
That is the Show (Berio) Ballet Rambert
Photo: Alan Cunliffe

RIGHT John Chesworth (b. 1930)
Pawn to King 5 (Pink Floyd) Ballet Rambert
Gideon Avrahami, Sandra Craig
Photo: Anthony Crickmay

'*H*', a manifesto in movement about the H-bomb, and *Pawn to King 5*, to music by a pop group, Pink Floyd, in which he indicated the infectious nature of violence in society with images drawn from discotheque dancing, a portrait of a wounded soldier and a Kabuki-style ritual suicide. Chesworth later became director in succession to Morrice, with Christopher Bruce, Rambert's best male dancer, as chief choreographer. Bruce's most notable productions have been *Wings*, using dance images of birds as predators and scavengers far removed from ballet's usual swan-queens; an expression of the waste of war, *for these who die as cattle*; and a series of works to music by the American

ABOVE Christopher Bruce (b. 1945)
Wings (Bob Downes) Ballet Rambert
Jonathan Taylor, Gideon Avrahami, Joseph Scoglio
Photo: Anthony Crickmay

OVERLEAF Merce Cunningham
Un jour ou deux (Cage) Paris Opéra Ballet
Jessica Sordoillet, Jean-Paul Gravier rehearsing
Photo: François Hers

composer George Crumb. Bruce was involved also in producing, jointly
with the mime Lindsay Kemp, a spectacle based on García Lorca's life
and work, *Cruel Garden*. With these and other creations, some by
American guests, the Rambert policy has swung to being in practice a
modern dance company.

Even such a monument of classical tradition as the Ballet of the Paris
Opéra has introduced modern elements into its activity. Cage and
Cunningham created a long work for its dancers, *Un jour ou deux*; an
experimental group was set up under the American modern dancer
Carolyn Carlson which has produced mainly mixed-media work; and

83

Tetley created *Tristan* at the Opéra to a score by Hans Werner Henze with Nureyev and Carlson in the leads. But that company's work remains primarily classical, although suffering from the lack of a resident choreographer.

The Royal Ballet, too, flirted with modernist experiment for a while in the early 1970s when Kenneth MacMillan became director, but somewhat half-heartedly and not for long. More sustained was the attempt Flemming Flindt made to broaden the work of the Royal Danish Ballet during his period as director (1966–78). Taylor, Tetley, the younger American choreographer Lar Lubovitch and the older Antony Tudor all came to mount existing ballets for the company, and another American modern dancer, Murray Louis, created *Cleopatra* for them. But the most important new production in this line was by Flindt himself. His first ballet, *The Lesson*, had been a translation into movement of a play by Ionesco, about an apparently mild teacher who kills

LEFT
Flemming Flindt (b. 1936)
The Lesson (Delerue)
Western Theatre Ballet
Simon Mottram,
Arlette van Boven
Photo: Anthony Crickmay

OPPOSITE
Flemming Flindt
The Triumph of Death
(Koppel)
Royal Danish Ballet

his pupil when carried away by the power he acquires over her. A less-known play by Ionesco was the source of *The Triumph of Death*, in which a rock score specially written for the group Savage Rose accompanied a macabre danced drama showing modern man trying vainly to escape from a plague. As with *Mutations*, a couple of episodes involving nudity caught the headlines, but equally notable was the way Flindt used images of modern life (a man jogging, a husband coming home from work) in his drama, and the moving duet he created for two older dancers as a grey-haired couple dying in the littered streets where dust-carts collected the corpses. *The Triumph of Death* brought the company a new audience, but it represented only one side of their work, and of Flindt's, because he also produced for them an entertaining *Nutcracker* on wholly traditional lines and a highly popular recreation of one of Bournonville's lost ballets, *The Toreador*.

The changes in ballet noted so far sprang mainly from influences

within the art itself by a process of cross-fertilization. But no art exists in a vacuum, and dance has been equally changed by new ideas in the other arts or in society as a whole. Think of the clothes people wore, the books they read, movies they watched and music they listened to even a few years ago. In spite of the recent trend towards nostalgic revival of old (and not-so-old) fashion, all have changed. So, in the same way, has ballet.

The biggest change has been the discovery of a new way of conveying meaning. Once a film would have needed to explain who its characters were, where they were and why; now directors can leave more to the imagination. Novelists, too, often see no need to explain their situation or characters. Even a necessarily simple art like pop music uses lyrics which would have seemed incomprehensible to a previous generation, and the theatre shows the same tendency. It became apparent, for instance, in *Hair*, although the more sensational aspects of that show stole most of the comment. The authors of the original play asked Tom Horgan, when he directed it, to cut out the spoken dialogue as far as possible in order to make it as little like a conventional musical as could be. Yet *Hair* did not end up without a plot; it merely conveyed the situation and its development by the music, lyrics and stage action without need for an explicit story-line. More recently, *A Chorus Line* similarly made its effects more by song and dance than by dialogue. Increasingly it has become true, if not that 'the medium is the message', at least that the message of any work of art can be expressed only in its own medium. Marshal McLuhan's famous phrase crystallized what people were already thinking.

In a way, it has always been true that ballet makes its points best through the emotional implications of the dancing itself. You learn more about Princess Aurora in *The Sleeping Beauty* from her solos and from the big adagio in each act of the ballet than from the mime episodes between them, but even so the mime was a necessary part of the ballet's structure. Nowadays choreographers manage without. Tetley's career illustrates the process of change. His early ballets, though expressed in dance images rather than explicit acting, contained a clear theme: man as victim, destroyer and discoverer in *The Anatomy Lesson*, for instance, where you had specific figures of mother, wife and child. Later, content was refined away to the extent that it could not easily or exactly be put into words, although still intelligible to the spectator. In *Mythical Hunters* the dances contained images of hunting, flight and capture: this became a metaphor for the relationship of men and women, then (by each captive prey giving birth to a successor) an image of the generations. In his more recent *Greening*, the whole content is implied in the original subtitle, 'Waiting for rain.'

Some choreographers have always preferred to imply, not state, their meaning. Paul Taylor is one such (the circlings, the mournings, the mysterious substitution of one dancer for another in *Runes* are characteristic). In Tudor's *The Leaves are fading*, the transitory nature of youth is only gently implied by an older woman who crosses the stage alone before and after the series of duets that make up the main action. Van Manen, when he allows drama into his choreography, generally leaves its meaning to the audience to imagine for themselves (as if you saw people through a window and could not hear their conversation), but in *Grand Trio*, a ballet to Schubert's music, a definite relationship is firmly conveyed between two of the characters within a framework of plotless dances for the rest of the cast. His duet *Twilight* is in one sense a modern equivalent of the traditional pas de deux, with entrée, adagio, solos and coda. But it takes place in front of an industrial cityscape and the woman wears a short dress, with high-heeled shoes which she removes after a time. Those facts, the strange nervousness of Cage's music for prepared piano and the edginess of the choreography itself give the dance a fierce and sensuous flavour suggesting a relationship between lovers who cannot be happy together or apart.

Another important change has been in what is regarded as the acceptable nature of dancing. One factor blurring the edges has been the increased interest of some visual artists in 'performance art' where they arrange a tableau or activity instead of painting a picture or making a sculpture. Many theatre people, too, became interested in multi-media activities where speech, movement, music and other arts were set to complement each other in less formally structured ways than would have been thought to constitute a play or a musical. It was only natural that choreographers should claim a comparable freedom to cross old boundaries.

A further factor in this development was the influence of the performers and creators who came together during the 1960s in a hall made available in Judson Church, New York. The Judson Dance Theatre had no director, its decisions were reached by common consent. Robert Dunn, a composer married to a dancer, Judith Dunn, taught composition courses, and people from widely differing backgrounds were allowed scope to try out their ideas. Creators like James Waring, Remy Charlip, Yvonne Rainer, Steve Paxton had original ideas and the 'anything goes' spirit allowed a tremendous burst of creative energy.

Glen Tetley
Mythical Hunters (Partos)
Netherlands Dance Theatre
Photo: Rosemary Winckley

That carried over into Grand Union, a group started in 1970 by several fine dancers, including a number previously with Cunningham. Performing at intervals with varying groups of dancers, they worked by improvisation which was given cohesiveness by the close relationship of the individual (and often very individualistic) artists with each other as part of an informal community.

Rather different is another kind of improvisation which began to be practised during the 1970s – contact improvisation, where two or more

Hans van Manen
Twilight (Cage)
Dutch National Ballet
Alexandra Radius,
Han Ebbelaar
Photo: Jorge Fatauros

dancers would respond in performance to the chance ways their bodies came together in movement.

With this background, the developing choreographers, especially in the United States, felt a freedom to try whatever they wished. Some pursued esoteric paths, like Stephanie Evanitsky who invented aero-dance, where the dancers move through harnesses hung from scaffolding: an idea that sounds precious and silly but in fact can achieve beautiful, amusing and dramatic effects. The dancers of Pilobolus base

93

their work primarily on gymnastics, and several people have tried to perform choreography made by computers, which generally proves extremely boring.

Dan Wagoner created several of his dances in collaboration with a poet, George Montgomery; his solo *Brambles* is performed in an imaginary décor merely described by Montgomery. One of Wagoner's duets is danced at first by the light of a single candle which is later blown out so that the audience can hear and sense the movements but cannot see them. Senta Driver, who (like Wagoner) made her name in Taylor's company before starting on her own, made one dance where the performer remains seated throughout and another where she accompanies her repeated circuits of the stage by speaking a roll-call of great dancers of the past.

More in the mainstream, although also using speech in some of his dances, is Louis Falco, a former Limón dancer. He has made works for Netherlands Dance Theatre, the French Ballet-Théâtre Contemporain and Ballet Rambert, as well as his own company. In some of them the dancers talk to each other while dancing: *Sleepers* is one such, and *Journal* another, the conversations being invented extempore by the dancers in the course of the initial rehearsals. Falco's characteristic style is fast and energetic, and titles such as *Caviar* or *Champagne* reflect a frank love of the pleasures of life which manifests itself in the manner of his ballets and the style of his company. Several of his dancers, notably Jennifer Muller and Juan Antonio, have in turn become interesting choreographers.

Twyla Tharp, after dancing first with Taylor, began her choreographic career with a strongly experimental bias: in one dance she dropped a ball, which bounced, then an egg, which did not, thus demonstrating something about the nature of movement. With *Eight Jelly Rolls* and *The Bix Pieces*, she admitted to her work the elements of jazz, tap, baton-twirling and social dance. This often gives it a flippant surface, beneath which lies a meticulous craftsmanship and perfectionism; every apparently casual gesture is planned and rehearsed with infinite care. Her own performing style is marked by tense energy, which she generally contrasts with the gentler suavity of another of the dancers. The musical base of her works has more than once set classical music in juxtaposition with ragtime, paralleling the mixture of choreographic styles. Two works created for the Joffrey Ballet and, even more, *Push comes to Shove*, which she created for American Ballet Theatre with Mikhail Baryshnikov in the lead, have made her talent more widely known and established her as a leader in her field.

It was a logical consequence of the experiments taking place in the form and content of dance that the kind of music used and the visual design of costumes and setting should also change. Traditional melodies and conventional frilled dresses are unlikely to suit ballets that seriously aim to say something about life today. Rock music has been mentioned in connection with several works, but dance has done much for serious modern music too. Merce Cunningham particularly was a

Twyla Tharp (b. 1942)
Unidentified work

pioneer in this respect: the first presentation of *musique concrète* in the United States was his solo *Collage*, to an extract from Pierre Schaeffer's *Symphonie pour un homme seul* (a score which Béjart also used), and Cunningham's *Suite by chance* was the first dance work with a pure electronic sound score, commissioned from Christian Wolff. His collaboration with John Cage has been consistent and close. That makes some of his work difficult for an uninitiated audience to accept, even when Cage is in his most benign mood, such as the 'score' for *How to pass, kick, fall and run* which consists of a speaker (usually Cage himself) sitting at one side of the stage and reading highly entertaining anecdotes from one of his books to a stop-watch timing.

But although the use of modern music sometimes makes life harder for the choreographers and dancers, it is observable that even the most difficult modern music becomes easier to follow when it is accompanied by relevant movement. And the music for its part can lead a choreographer into paths he might not otherwise have followed: for instance, in Jaap Flier's ballet to György Ligeti's *Nouvelles aventures*, where the dancers explore a limbo of the soul before finding themselves squashed ignominiously by the droppings of the gods. One of the early successes of London Contemporary Dance Theatre was *Vesalii Icones*, conceived by the composer Peter Maxwell Davies as a work for cello solo, small instrumental group and dancer (who also has to play the piano). With its action based jointly on the anatomical engravings of the sixteenth century physician Vesalius and on the Stations of the Cross, the task of the choreographer and dancer William Louther was facilitated by the composer's specific recommendations.

Many other composers have become interested, even eager, to write for dance. In Britain at least, that is helped by the availability of public and private funds for commissioning scores. A further attraction to composers is that their work is certain to get a hearing, which is not always the case for an unknown musician, and that it may well have many performances, which is unusual even for leading contemporary composers in the concert hall.

The relationship between music and dance has changed too. At one time it was taken for granted that music was the starting point of the ballet. Nowadays they are often independent, the music no more closely related to the dance than the décor is. Dancing in silence, a great novelty as little as 30 years ago, is commonplace. This is sometimes argued as demonstrating the increased strength of dance, that it no longer needs a prop; but it has yet to be proved that dances made in this

Jaap Flier (b. 1934)
Nouvelles aventures (Ligeti) Netherlands Dance Theatre
Lenny Westerdijk
Photo: Anthony Crickmay

way are as durable as those which follow older methods.

Design for ballet has changed too, though partly for different reasons. An economic factor is that ballet can be danced in the simplest costumes with no setting. This is sometimes a positive advantage: Balanchine's ballets, for instance, often look best with the dancers in practice clothes (tights and leotard or singlet) so that nothing distracts from the choreography. At the other extreme, there has sometimes seemed to be a contest between designers to achieve the most grandiose setting for classic revivals. In general, however, the tendency has been towards simplicity and solidity.

Martha Graham pioneered the use of sculpture in the designing of ballets and this has proved remarkably successful. Screens, cut-outs, projections, scaffolding and other objects have become more common, realistic painted backcloths less so. Texture, colour and shape are the qualities that matter. The aim is to provide an environment for the dance rather than a moving picture. Isamu Noguchi, Alex Katz, William Katz, Rouben Ter-Arutunian and Cunningham's collaborators are among those who have been most influential in America, and Ralph Koltai, Nadine Baylis and Nicholas Georgiadis in Europe.

In costume, the changes have been equally striking. The early modern dancers used the stretchable qualities of jersey knit and bias-cut fabrics to special effect and this still sometimes continues. But in general, the clothes dancers wear in modern works have tended to become more like those they wear off-stage, or alternatively to be reduced to a bare minimum.

As designs became simpler, lighting grew more ambitious. Jean Rosenthal in America first introduced effects with low side lighting to pick out the individual dancers from surrounding darkness. Others, branching out from her discoveries, have made stage lighting an art of its own. When Rauschenberg was artistic director for Cunningham, one of the aspects he was most concerned with was the lighting.

The extent to which design and lighting could become almost a primary art in themselves is shown by the Alwin Nikolais Dance Theatre of New York. Nikolais, who is choreographer, designer and composer for his own works, often conceals his dancers in costumes that completely hide the body's shape, and uses tricks of lighting (with unusual colours, or alternating areas of light and darkness so that a dancer can seem to appear and disappear) so ingeniously that it becomes a part, and sometimes apparently the major part, of the ballet's effect.

Alwin Nikolais (b. 1912)
Somniloquy (Nikolais) Nikolais Dance Theatre
Photo: Susan Schiff-Faludi

New stages, new audiences

It is claimed that for every ticket sold in 1965 for a professional dance performance in the United States, sixteen tickets were sold in 1975. Other parts of the world have not reached that rate of growth but there has been an enormous world-wide expansion of dance activity over recent years. Consequently, for every company or choreographer who is mentioned in this book for some special merit, innovation or significance, there are many others working away, sometimes unnoticed except by their local audiences.

Within the United States alone there are between forty and fifty professional ballet companies and nearly two hundred professional modern dance companies or groups. In addition there are hundreds of regional, civic or college companies working on an amateur basis; the *Dance Magazine* Annual lists more than three hundred, and those are just the ones that replied to questionnaires. Some of these companies have high standards, but even the worst of them must reflect some public interest in dance among the community they serve.

The phenomenon known as 'regional ballet' has been gathering strength ever since it first crystallized at a regional ballet festival held in Atlanta, Georgia, in 1956. The term indicates a non-professional company (usually based on a dance school or group of schools) which regularly appears before paying audiences in works that are serious in intent even if limited in scope. They serve to keep interest alive and sometimes to provide students with useful experience before starting a professional career. The practice seems not to have been copied much outside the United States but there are a few instances elsewhere, even in Britain where emphasis on regionalism in the arts is a comparatively recent development.

The Soviet Union also has continued to expand the number of its ballet companies, reaching at least three dozen major professional ones in addition to amateur troupes and others attached to operetta theatres. Several of them have appeared in the west: two from Moscow, two from Leningrad and one each from Kiev, Novosibirsk, Perm and Tbilisi. Dancers from others have been seen as guest artists or on concert programmes: enough of them to make clear that the general standard is reasonably high even though (as would be expected) it does vary. The Novosibirsk Ballet is an example of one formed fairly recently to meet the needs of a developing neighbourhood. Dancers were sent from elsewhere to start it off, including some promising soloists from the Kirov, and guest choreographers went to mount works for the initial repertory. In fact it was not long before Novosibirsk developed its own choreographer, Oleg Vinogradov, who won a considerable reputation, was invited to work also in Moscow and Leningrad, and has now become director of the Kirov Ballet.

Russia does not have such companies as some of the leading American ones (including Ballet Theatre and the Joffrey) which depend for their continuance on touring for most of the year. They do sometimes show their work outside their home town but for the most part serve a particular theatre in a regional capital. In this their American equivalent might be, say, the San Francisco Ballet, long established and with a high reputation for the quality of its dancers, many of whom have later graduated elsewhere. During the 1960s there was a conscious effort, with large grants from the Ford Foundation, to build up other companies of superior quality outside New York; the Pennsylvania Ballet is perhaps the one to have made most progress although its creative achievements so far are modest.

The question of grants is important as it is increasingly difficult to run a large-scale dance company without some kind of financial support. In America grants are generally provided by the big foundations or by tax-exempt endowments, and in recent years by the dance programme of the National Endowment for the Arts. But such grants are usually made on condition of matching them dollar for dollar (and sometimes even higher ratios) from box office earnings and private donations. In Britain and some British Commonwealth countries there are state-financed Arts Councils; elsewhere, subsidy generally comes from municipal or state support.

Occasionally, still, private support can be on an exceptional scale. Its possibilities and limitations are both illustrated by the history of the Harkness Ballet started in 1965 by Rebekah Harkness, who had previously aided several other companies through the Foundation of which she was president. Her company had fine dancers but the repertory scarcely displayed them to great advantage. The best works in the early days were inherited, with several of the dancers, from one of Mrs Harkness's former beneficiaries, the Robert Joffrey Ballet. This company, founded by Joffrey on a small scale, had grown over the years and made many successful tours including one to Russia, but had to close when it lost the Harkness backing which it had come to rely on. Luckily for Joffrey, he was able to revive his company later with other funds and went on to fresh strength. The Harkness Ballet was less fortunate. In 1970 it was suddenly disbanded and its name given instead to its associated Youth Company; that in turn had to be ended in 1975 when stock market changes diminished Mrs Harkness's fortune.

Luckily the prestige that can be won for a country or a city by its arts helps to ensure that support, once granted, generally continues. Even countries with no previous traditions of ballet have started companies, although the significance they have outside their own area depends more on the talents of those running them than on the material resources. Thus Holland, in which ballet did not really establish itself until the end of the 1940s, has come to occupy a prime place in European ballet, with two companies of international standard and several choreographers much in demand outside. Germany has built up a similarly widespread interest in ballet over much the same period; almost every town has a dance company attached to its leading theatre, although their quality and importance varies immensely. The arrival of a new director to take over a company can bring a complete transformation, as John Neumeier's arrival in first Frankfurt, then Hamburg, or Pina Bausch's in Wuppertal.

Other countries which have established companies in recent years, for motives varying from national pride to the aggrandisement of a ruler include Iran, The Philippines, Venezuela. Israel has formed two modern dance companies which have toured extensively abroad, and others at home too. Belgium has two large companies with royal charters in addition to Béjart's famous company in Brussels; they are based in Charleroi and Antwerp and serve primarily the Walloon and Flemish areas respectively. Cuba under Castro, thanks largely to the presence of a distinguished ballerina, Alicia Alonso, supports three companies.

Turkey, in contrast to some countries which tried to start a company at once, began with a school and now has companies in Ankara and Istanbul. Canada, where the first professional ballet company dates only from 1939, now has three major classical companies and many modern dance groups. Australia in recent years has built up a national ballet with fine dancers and an eclectic repertory, as well as companies of reputable standard and lively policy serving the individual states. Vast distances separate them, but at a festival held in 1978 at Sydney to enable them to exchange ideas, Australian Dance Theatre won much admiration for Jonathan Taylor's comic *Flibbertigibbet*, and Graeme

Jonathan Taylor (b. 1941)
Flibbertigibbet (Bach) Australian Dance Theatre
Margaret Wilson, Joseph Scoglio
Photo: David B. Simmonds

Murphy's *Rumours* for the Dance Company (New South Wales) showed a bold mind, and outstanding local talent in music and décor.

It might be thought that public funding as a major source of income would discourage experiment, but that is not by any means invariably true. In fact there are examples of 'official' companies specifically started for the sake of experiment. The Sopiane Ballet at Pecs in Hungary began in that way; Ballet Prague flourished for a time with its base in the subsidized Theatre Studio there; in Leningrad and Moscow there have been similar attempts.

The country that has probably done most to pour public money into experimental dance is France, sometimes but not always through the work of the Maisons de la Culture which were set up to bring art, and especially modern art, to the regions, so that wider sections of the public could share what was formerly a minority privilege. Ballet-Théâtre Contemporain was founded, based first at Amiens, then at Angers, to devote itself entirely to new work based on twentieth-century music; it also made use of notable painters and sculptors including Sonia Delaunay and Alexander Calder. Reorganization as Ballet-Théâtre Français and a new base at Nancy has lately brought a slightly more eclectic policy, but it remains adventurous and has introduced, for instance, choreography by Carolyn Brown and Viola Farber, two former partners of Merce Cunningham, both of whom work within his tradition; also by Louis Falco, all of them collaborating with American composers and designers. At Nancy the company displaced Gheorghe Caciuleanu, a young Romanian choreographer with a distinctive if somewhat unruly talent, but he in turn found fresh sponsorship to establish a new small company with the title Théâtre Chorégraphique at Rennes. Meanwhile, in the studios at Angers formerly occupied by Ballet-Théâtre Contemporain, Alwin Nikolais was given funds by the state and the city to set up a modern dance school from which a French national modern dance company will shortly be formed.

At the other extreme, artists without official backing have found ingenious ways to present their work. Judson Church in New York, already mentioned, is only one example of the way unlikely buildings have been pressed into use: former warehouses and army drill halls, lofts and basements, school halls and cathedral naves are just a few. In

Pavel Smok (b. 1927)
Gangrene (Mingus) Ballet Prague

104

Gheorge Caciuleanu (b. 1947)
Founambulis (de Falla) Théâtre Chorégraphique de Rennes
Ruxandra Racovitza, Gheorge Caciuleanu

OPPOSITE Carolyn Brown (b. 1927)
Balloon (Brown) Ballet-Théâtre Contemporain
Photo: Pierre Petitjean

this way, a proliferation of new small companies and groups, mainly of modern dancers, has been able to come into existence in America, Britain and France at least, and to some extent elsewhere too.

Dance has also been taken up by minority groups. In New York, the black dancer Arthur Mitchell, after a distinguished career as a principal in Balanchine's company, felt a need to give something back to the community he had come from. Starting with dance classes for young people as a social benefit, he went on to form a classical ballet company entirely of black dancers, Dance Theatre of Harlem. There had been previous attempts on such lines, and Alvin Ailey's Dance Theatre had always been predominantly though not exclusively black. Mitchell however was the first to adopt a classical repertory including a number of Balanchine's ballets, and although he had to push some of his soloists beyond their capacity, the results were impressive. As a student, when given a scholarship to the School of American Ballet, Mitchell was warned that because of his colour he would have to be twice as good as a white dancer if he were to get into a white company. Later, when challenged about the Harlem company's discriminatory exclusiveness, he said he would be glad to admit white dancers on equal terms once other companies did the same for black dancers who have so far found very limited opportunities in classical companies, although perhaps the situation has grown a little easier over the years.

A more questionable development has been the formation of 'drag ballets', in which all the women's roles are taken by men in wigs, make-up, tutus and toe-shoes. Two such troupes, both with the name Trockadero in their title, have enjoyed a vogue in the United States in spite of an approach which fell somewhere between mockery and imitation of ballerinas and ballets.

Among all the attempts to bring ballet to the greatest number of people, the obvious opportunities presented by television and film have remained comparatively little developed. The few feature films that have been made are usually of stage ballets performed by famous stars, and either photographed straight or adapted in only the most perfunctory way. They are shown repeatedly, however, on the art cinema circuits, demonstrating a real demand, and *The Turning Point* (like *The Red Shoes* long before) proved the possibilities of a massive box-office appeal. But no really successful film has yet been made of a ballet specifically designed for the screen.

In television, there have been some useful experiments. Alwin Nikolais prepared some works specially for television, incorporating effects feasible only with the aid of multiple cameras and electronic devices. Peter Darrell, in two ballets for BBC-television, explored the idea that, on the small screen, simple movement based on a dancer's sense of rhythm and timing looked better than choreography using technique developed for the stage. His subjects, prepared by a playwright, John Hopkins, were too esoteric for mass appeal: *Orpheus* saw the hero as a pop star and Eurydice as a beautiful model girl. But the results were far from negligible. Robert Cohan, too, has made some special television ballets for London Contemporary Dance Theatre.

Considering how many more people can see ballet on film or television than on stage, it seems astonishing that the problems of translating

Peter Darrell
A Man like Orpheus (Leppard) Western Theatre Ballet for BBC television
Suzanne Hywel, Peter Cazalet

dance into this different medium have met with little attention and even less success. A few producers (among them a former dancer, Margaret Dale, in Britain, and Manfred Gräter in Germany) have found ways of effecting a reasonable compromise to show stage ballets on the screen, and the more widespread use of colour television has brought an improvement. But there is a vast field still open for whoever evolves ways of creating works satisfactorily from scratch for the large or small screen. Even when this is achieved, it will be a supplement rather than a rival to live performances with their immediacy of contact between performer and spectator, but even with that limitation, it remains worth trying.

Meanwhile, ballet on stage goes on finding new and larger audiences. In this, a few celebrated stars play a part (as they have done throughout ballet's history) in drawing the crowds, and also in establishing the public interest that can benefit other performers too. Stars are not new, but some of the present ways of producing them are. Whereas Pavlova toured with her own supporting company in regular ballets, there has grown up a fashion for gala programmes in which a series of leading dancers give their party-pieces. More artistically satisfying is the type of programme Nureyev has pioneered under the title 'Nureyev and Friends' in which a small specially assembled cast of soloists and principals dance works not needing a corps de ballet. Another development in presentation associated with him has been the establishment of annual 'Nureyev Festivals' in London and Paris, and similar seasons on Broadway, when he dances with several different supporting companies in succession over a period of weeks. This has had more than commercial significance, because he has used the seasons to have new works commissioned, and they have also given opportunities to visiting companies to appear in guest engagements which they would not otherwise have been offered. At a time when the disproportionately increasing cost of travel makes international touring more difficult, this has served as a valuable, though necessarily limited, corrective.

New men, new women

We have been looking mainly at trends and tendencies, although with an eye to the extent to which they can be started or influenced by gifted individuals. To guess what further changes may come is usually unprofitable, but some clues can be found in the work of those creative people who have come into a dominant position during the past decade.

Bear in mind that, while promising newcomers arrive and sometimes quickly depart again, the true craftsmen go on for a long time, as is shown by the careers of Bournonville and Petipa in the last century, Ashton and Balanchine in this. What the two old masters create still has more drawing power than the work of most of their juniors, and often (through the courage and accumulated wisdom of experience) more originality too.

Exceptional talent, even if it rebels against its sources, is most likely to appear where there is a lively tradition to foster its growth; not necessarily a long tradition, since that can lose its energy. Occasionally an interesting choreographer emerges from a background not much noted for dance, as Oscar Araiz did from Buenos Aires, but even there may be found a large, although not very creative, ballet company, and Araiz was also influenced by a modern dancer from Germany, Dore Hoyer, who settled there for some years. Araiz has worked for leading companies in Hamburg, Paris, New York and Winnipeg, as well as with his own Argentine company. His response to music has provoked extremes of admiration and ridicule, and he has produced both highly individual treatments of Mahler's songs and also Prokofiev's *Romeo and Juliet* with three dancers representing different aspects of the heroine.

On the whole, modern dance has kept a creative lead over classical ballet, with the proviso that, although it has produced more of the best choreographers, it has also produced more of the worst, thanks to the belief (encouraged often by training methods which include dance composition classes) that it is almost their duty to create as well as perform. On the whole, too, modern dance in the United States remains more innovative and more accomplished than in Europe, and not only because there is so much more happening there. Standards of expectation are higher too, because of the inevitable comparison with past accomplishments.

Several of the leading practitioners, including some still making their names, have already been mentioned. Another who has come to the top is Murray Louis, partly because of his own exceptional skill as a performer; lately he has augmented his reputation through an association with Nureyev, for whom he has made two ballets (one serious, one comic) and a solo. Formerly one of Nikolais's dancers, Louis still has his works lit by Nikolais, but he has made a more interesting use of music than his master, drawing from pop sources and the classics, and is more inventive of movement too, with a special flair for wit in the dances themselves as well as the subjects of his works.

Many of the young generation in America have turned away from the idea of subjects at all. Laura Dean has built dances on the hypnotic effect of repetitive movement patterns. Lucinda Childs in recent dances has repeated over and over again a simple and limited range of steps, such as just running, skipping and jumping, back and forwards along a diagonal or curve, with infinite tiny modifications of detail to provide a focus. Douglas Dunn is another of the most interesting among the many who have followed formalist paths to seek the theatrical qualities of pure movement without content.

Radically different approaches are shown by two women prominent in advanced American dance. Meredith Monk uses many elements other than dance in her presentations, works often in buildings other than theatres but aims at a strongly theatrical effect. Kei Takei's career began in Japan but was substantially modified by study in New York.

Oscar Araiz (b. 1940)
Romeo and Juliet (Prokofiev) Joffrey Ballet
Gary Chryst, Russell Sultzbach
Photo: Jack Mitchell

Douglas Dunn (b. 1942)
Photo: Peter Philipp

Murray Louis (b. 1926)
Moment (Ravel)
Louis Dance Company
Rudolf Nureyev
Photo: Rosemary Winckley

Louis Falco (b. 1942)
Cooking French (Alcantara)
Ballet-Théâtre Contemporain
Photo: Pierre Petitjean

Her works include ritual activities, based on everyday life but often obscure in their implications, mixed with sometimes painful movement such as that of a man repeatedly throwing himself to the floor. Her work has no narrative but a juxtaposition of happenings as in a collage. Many of her productions are parts of a series called *Light*, its first nine parts brought together in 1975 for a consecutive performance lasting seven hours.

These modern dance creators are only representative, by no means exhaustive. They and many others are working in a context where Cunningham and Graham are still creatively active, Paul Taylor no

longer dancing but going to new strength in his choreography, Louis Falco and Twyla Tharp, notably, thriving among the younger generation. The classical ballet scene in America, except for New York City Ballet, is altogether less healthy as far as creation is concerned, although it presents a flourishing surface thanks to the quality of the dancing and the importation of works from elsewhere.

American Ballet Theatre does have Tudor as an associate director, but in recent years he has made only two new ballets for them, adding prestige but able to refresh the repertory to only a limited extent. Several productions by Tetley included only two small ones which were entirely new, the rest being all revivals. Like other companies in America and elsewhere, Ballet Theatre has tried out new choreographers but without much success.

Almost the only American choreographer to make a name for himself in ballet lately is Eliot Feld, who began with Ballet Theatre but preferred to run his own company. His first attempt, the American Ballet

BELOW Eliot Feld (b. 1942)
Harbinger (Prokofiev) American Ballet Theatre

OPPOSITE Eliot Feld
At Midnight (Mahler) American Ballet Theatre
Bruce Marks

Company, proved too costly to keep going because he insisted on live music; the later Eliot Feld Ballet has coped by choosing a high proportion of music that does not need an orchestra, and otherwise making do with tapes. Although Feld made his name with the plotless, lively *Harbinger* and the moody, atmospheric *At Midnight*, to big scores by Prokofiev and Mahler, some of his best work has been done to piano music – *Intermezzo* (Brahms) and *A Footstep of Air* (Beethoven) both benefit from an intimate scale and light touch. But providing almost the entire repertory single-handed has led Feld often to adopt styles reminiscent of other choreographers instead of always developing the individuality found in his best ballets.

With the American example of how rarely good choreographers appear, the modest creative achievements of Russian ballet in recent

years can be understood. Within the USSR, potential talent is likely to direct itself towards classical ballet for lack of a modern dance alternative, but official preferences for work that is easily understood are equally a limitation.

Yuri Grigorovich, initially (and still by intent though not in achievement) an innovator, has directed the Bolshoi Ballet since 1964. He repeated in *Spartacus* the success he enjoyed with *The Stone Flower* of rehabilitating a score, this time by Khachaturian, that had failed in previous productions; again his solution was to reorganize the plot and to treat in terms of dancing what had previously been the subject of heavy acting. But subsequent ballets, in spite of providing some powerful roles (*Ivan the Terrible*, for instance), have come more to repeat a formula than to find new ideas.

Nikolai Boyarchikov has built a reputation first at the Maly Theatre, Leningrad, then in Perm. His *Romeo and Juliet* (mounted also in West Berlin) is an almost abstract treatment, with the story pared to a minimum. Oleg Vinogradov, who followed Boyarchikov at the Maly, has also produced a highly unconventional treatment of *Romeo and Juliet*, starting and finishing with the entire company in white tights for an ensemble from which the principals emerge to put on their costumes. The intention is to give the drama a sense of universality and the effect is not unlike Béjart in approach. Vinogradov's repertory includes also *Yaroslavna*, a dance treatment of the campaign that forms the subject of Borodin's opera *Ivan the Terrible*, but seen from the viewpoint of the women suffering at home during the war.

Two choreographers with closely similar names have created ballets at the Bolshoi. Vladimir Vassiliov, a former character dancer, has made a number of works in collaboration with his wife Natalia Kasatkina; the best known is probably *The Creation of the World*, a comic-strip parody created for the Kirov Ballet. More significant, perhaps, is the choreography of Vladimir Vassiliev, the company's heroic leading dancer. In *Icarus* he tried to use the myth as the basis of an allegory on the eternal need for individual effort; his choreographic invention did not equal his ambitious scope (and Yuri Slonimski's music even less so), but it was an interesting failure.

Yuri Grigorovich
Spartacus (Khachaturian) Bolshoi Ballet
Maris Liepa
Photo: A. Makarova

László Seregi (b. 1929)
Spartacus (Khachaturian) Australian Ballet
Gary Norman
Photo: Peter Barr

László Seregi, since 1977 director of the Hungarian Ballet, is in a more fortunate position, in that his predecessors had carefully built up links with both Russia and the west, getting the best of both worlds. That has enabled him to experiment more freely in ballets ranging from a tragic reading of *Spartacus* to a comic *Sylvia*, taking in also an idiosyncratic interpretation of Hindemith's *Kammermusik No 1* as a struggle for dominance in the course of a duet for two strong young ballerinas, Ildikó Pongor and Katalin Csarnoy.

After Ashton, the senior British choreographers are Peter Darrell and Kenneth MacMillan. Darrell, since 1969, has devoted himself to building up a national ballet in Scotland based on a nucleus from the former Western Theatre Ballet. His own creations have been to some extent subordinated to the need for a balanced repertory appealing to a relatively inexperienced audience, but the series of full-evening narrative ballets he has staged has shown invariably an original theatrical flair, *Tales of Hoffmann* particularly having established itself through the strong roles it offers its dancers.

MacMillan directed the Royal Ballet from 1970 until 1978 but it was not an entirely happy appointment and he asked to be relieved of it to

Kenneth MacMillan
Mayerling (Liszt) Royal Ballet
Wendy Ellis, David Wall
Photo: Anthony Crickmay

concentrate on choreography. His long-story ballets too, such as *Manon* and *Mayerling*, have been popular, but his most distinctive choreography has been in more concentrated works, often dealing with pathological themes, such as *My Brother, My Sisters* and *Métaboles*, created respectively for Stuttgart and Paris. A question for his future is whether the two ways of working could be reconciled to get the best of each in one work.

Among new choreographers in Britain over the past decade, two have so far stood out. Jonathan Thorpe's early creations for Northern Ballet Theatre (a company founded in Manchester in 1969) showed an individual expressiveness with small casts which has not been entirely sustained in his more ambitious later productions. André Prokovsky started choreography for the small touring company, New London Ballet, which he founded with his ballerina-wife Galina Samsova in 1972. He showed a highly musical approach, at its most successful in a bravura display piece to Verdi music, *Vespri*, and an ability to create atmosphere too.

The considerable growth of dance in the German theatres has meant that many of the most interesting developments have happened there. One is that modern dance, after a period of eclipse in that country, made something of a comeback during the 1970s, particularly in the industrial area along the Rhine valley. In 1971 the company at the Cologne city theatres was reformed under the name Tanz-Forum with a collective leadership, initially of three choreographers, of whom Jochen Ulrich and Gray Veredon remain. With some guest choreographers too, notably from Ballet Rambert, they set out to build an entirely modern group. One notable production is Ulrich's *Walzerträume*, based on the lives of Johann Strauss's family, with a score by Kurt Schwertsik making modern use of old melodies. As well as the company's own productions, there is a modern dance festival each summer in which invited companies from other countries also take part. Also, under the auspices of the International Summer Academy of Dance held each year in the city, a biennial choreographic competition is held to encourage young creators.

Earlier attempts to revive the once famous Folkwang Ballet in nearby Essen came to nothing, but a performing group based on the Folkwang Studio of modern dance continues occasional performances. From this studio, by way of a spell in America, came Pina Bausch who in 1973 took over the direction of the ballet company at the Wuppertal opera house and reformed it as the Wuppertal Dance Theatre. Bausch first

Jochen Ulrich (b. 1944)
Waltz Dreams (Schwertsik) Tanz-Forum, Cologne
Photo: Gert Weigelt

attracted favourable attention with her entirely danced stagings of operas by Gluck. A violently primitive interpretation of *The Rite of Spring* followed as part of a complete Stravinsky evening in contrasted styles, then a double bill based on music by Kurt Weill and words by Brecht. Later productions include a highly original long work about a man obsessively listening to a tape of Bartók's *Bluebeard* and identifying it with his own emotional life. A stark, harsh production style gives Bausch's work a strong impact and she has built a company which, unusually, pays no attention at all to looks, only to personality and commitment.

Among the German classical companies, John Neumeier since 1973 has established the Hamburg Ballet as a rival to the previously unchallenged Stuttgart company. He began making ballets while himself a dancer at Stuttgart, and directed his own company at Frankfurt for four years before moving, with several of his dancers, to Hamburg. One of his achievements has been to develop the company as a strong ensemble. Many of his ballets are radical reinterpretations of existing scores: the hero of his *Swan Lake*, for instance, is Ludwig II of Bavaria, a contemporary of Tchaikovsky whose life presents various parallels with that of the composer. He has also shown a special interest in Mahler's music, choreographing the third and fourth symphonies, and among his large-scale productions are one based on the lives and music of Meyerbeer and Schumann (contemporaries and rivals) and a *Midsummer Night's Dream* which mixes barrel-organ tunes and atmospheric modern scores by Ligeti with the familiar Mendelssohn music to match the multiple layers of Shakespeare's play.

Holland, like Germany, has maintained its importance as a centre of important activity in dance. Besides the large companies there are several experimental groups, including that of Koert Stuyf, whose choreography has rewardingly explored the limits of slow motion, thanks to the infinitely subtle control and compelling personality of his dancer-wife, Ellen Edinoff.

Pina Bausch (b. 1940)
Bluebeard (Bartók) Wuppertal Dance Theatre
Monika Sagon, Jean Mindo
Photo: Gert Weigelt

OVERLEAF John Neumeier (b. 1942)
Third Symphony (Mahler) Hamburg Ballet
Photo: F. Peyer

The Dutch National Ballet, a large and well-endowed company, has been given a more definite character of its own over the past ten years or so with Rudi van Dantzig as director sharing the creative responsibilities with Hans van Manen and Toer van Schayk. The last-named designs most of Van Dantzig's ballets and has also made several choreographies of his own, the most successful being the apocalyptic *Before, during and after the party* and the grimly ironic *Pyrrhic Dances II*. He and Van Dantzig both reveal, in their ballets, a serious concern for the society in which they work; their *Painted birds* used film, mime and dance to make vivid the dangers of pollution and ended movingly with the entire company assembling on stage to sing a chorus from Bach's St Matthew Passion.

Toer van Schayk (b. 1936)
Pyrrhic Dances II (Lully and Philidor) Dutch National Ballet
Francis Sinceretti, Corrice Rijkuiter
Photo: Jorge Fatauros

Rudi van Dantzig (b. 1933)
Monument for a dead boy (Boerman) Dutch National Ballet
Rudolf Nureyev
Photo: Hans van den Busken

Van Dantzig's most famous ballet is *Monument for a dead boy*, vividly and compassionately expressing in flashback the life of a boy who died young. Besides using ballet technique in an original way, he has been consistent in using modern music to fine purpose, from his early Webern ballet, *Moments*, to his recent staging of Stockhausen's *Gesang der Jünglinge*.

Rudi van Dantzig
Gesang der Jünglinge
(Stockhausen)
Dutch National Ballet
Photo: Jorge Fatauros

Hans van Manen
5 Tangos (Piazolla) Dutch National Ballet
Photo: Jorge Fatauros

Balancing the dramatic works of those two are Van Manen's ballets. He acquired a mastery of pure classical form sometimes using unexpected music, such as the symphonic dances by a Brazilian composer, Astor Piazolli, for *5 Tangos*. Van Manen's interest in form and his highly innovative attitude combined to fine effect in *Live*, where a video-cameraman joined two dancers to achieve effects of contrast and viewpoint impossible without modern technology.

134

Hans van Manen
Live (Liszt) Dutch National Ballet
Coleen Davis
Photo: Jorge Fatauros

The other leading Dutch company, Netherlands Dance Theatre, after a period during which excessively experimental and mostly American productions brought it to a state of limited interest, has since 1976 regained its old quality under a young director, Jiri Kylián, whose ballets include a stirring display piece to Janáček's *Sinfonietta*. Most of his works have a specific content but not usually expressed as a story, rather with the allusive implications that give meaning to a painting, although with nothing static about them. In fact he introduces unusual movement qualities, including one dance in his *November Steps* which is performed on a sheet of material stretched at an angle across the stage. Kylián has also turned to creating choreography for television, in a work based on Janáček's *Intimate Letters*.

Although not much past 30, Kylián has already given too much evidence of his unusual creative talent to be dismissed as promising. He certainly will be one of the influential figures of the next decade. So, too, will his contemporary Richard Alston, the most talented choreographer

Jiri Kylián (b. 1947)
Intimate Letters (Janáček) Swedish TV
Gerd Andersson, Niklas Ek
Photo: Lesley Leslie-Spinks

to come so far from the London School of Contemporary Dance. Much of his early work was done for a group he formed under the name Strider, who worked so determinedly to keep renewing their ideas and subjecting themselves to new experiences that after a while he had to take a sabbatical, which he spent studying in New York. On his return to London he chose not to set up a regular company but to work intermittently with a group of very able dancers who also appear either as freelances or with other companies. Their creations have combined a rigorous interest in form with a cheerful informality of manner.

Jiri Kylián
November Steps (Takemitsu) Netherlands Dance Theatre
Photo: Tony van Muyden

Richard Alston (b. 1948)
Rainbow Bandit
(Amarkhanian)
London Contemporary
Dance Theatre
Tom Jobe
Photo: Anthony Crickmay

A Swedish choreographer, Ingegerd Lönnroth, has shown more than common ability in productions for the Junction Dance Company which she and Kris Donovan run with a base at the North London Polytechnic (one of the first British examples of the American practice of dance companies securing affiliation to an educational establishment). Also, after a long period during which the Royal Ballet conscientiously attempted, with little result, to give new choreographers a chance, they have at last found in David Bintley a very young man who can turn his hand to different kinds of ballet, express himself in distinctive movement and show off the talents of the dancers. At the same time, several students still at the Royal School have also demonstrated lively ideas and a skilled approach to choreography.

New York City Ballet, too, has shown choreography by one of its leading dancers, Peter Martins, which was made for a special occasion

but thought worth extending and taking into the repertory, giving hope of a substantial talent. Another distinguished male dancer who has already given ample evidence of choreographic ability is Rudolf Nureyev, with his new versions of the classics as well as his new interpretation of *Romeo and Juliet* for London Festival Ballet. It can only be a matter of time before he devotes himself more extensively to making new works.

Trained like Nureyev at the Kirov School in Leningrad, Valery Panov has lately turned to choreography with productions of *Cinderella* and *The Rite of Spring* in West Berlin, and a ballet based on *The Idiot* which showed real dramatic flair. Elsewhere in Germany, the Stuttgart Ballet has made the brave experiment of allowing no fewer than three of its dancers, who had shown promise in workshop productions, to create several works apiece in order to develop their ability. William Forsythe has gone furthest so far in establishing his merit as a result of this, even to the extent of mounting a big two-act ballet, *Orpheo*, to a specially composed score by Hans Werner Henze with a scenario by the playwright Edward Bond. At least one other of the aspirants, Rosemary Helliwell, showed an individuality that is likely to progress further; and at Stuttgart, too, there is a young dancer, Uwe Scholz, whose creative potential attracted comment even before he left the school.

Nobody ten years ago could have hoped to forecast more than a fraction of what has happened in dance during that time, and the next decade is equally unpredictable. The one thing that may be confidently expected is that with the number of new and old talents that are around, and the likelihood of others to come, all forms of ballet will remain as lively, as engaging, as changeable and enjoyable as they have proved in recent years.

George Balanchine
Episodes (Webern)
New York City Ballet
Patricia Neary
Photo: Iwamoto

Index

144